BASIC
BIBLE
TRUTHS

A PROVEN SOULWINNING METHOD

LESTER HUTSON

Basic Bible Truths

Cover Design by Dustin Myers

ISBN: 978-1-7324282-1-8

www.lesterhutson.org

Table of Contents

Foreword

The greatest need in America today is not being met in the Halls of Congress or from the benches of the Supreme Court. While our culture moves away from God, we can still win people to Christ one person at a time. The greatest need in America today is the simple plan of salvation. As Romans 10:14 reminds us, "How shall they hear without a preacher?"

The verse I have signed in Bibles for years is Acts 4:29: *"And now, Lord, behold their threatenings: and grant unto thy servants, that with all boldness they may speak thy word."* It is imperative that we raise up a generation that speaks boldly for the cause of Christ. Reaching the world for Christ should be the number one goal of every believer. I firmly believe that Christians be properly trained to witness. We are losing our children and our country as a whole because we have not successfully transferred out Christian faith to the next generation. It is critically important to teach others and disciple them in the Biblical faith.

During his lifetime of ministry, my friend Dr. Lester Hutson, has seen great success from the teaching in Basic Bible Truths. God began using Dr. Hutson at the young age of 14 to pastor a small church, and he has been actively serving the Lord for more than 50 years. What a privilege to see into the heart and learn from a man who has devoted his entire life to winning souls and teaching others to do the same.

I am privileged to call Dr. Hutson my friend, and I highly encourage you and your church to take hold to the principles used in this proven soul-winning tool.

Dr. David Gibbs, Jr.

i

From the Author

About 7:15 a.m. on Thursday morning, December 7, 1967, I met an oilfield work-over rig head-on at about thirty-five miles per hour. Miraculously, God let me live, but it took a long time to recover from the many breaks and cuts. During the first four months, while I was totally bedridden, God gave me the seed for this tremendous evangelism-discipleship tool. I had lots of time to think as I lay there; the progression of truths in Christianity which are set forth in this book began to take shape in my mind. I had long seen the need for such a short course as this, which could be used by the ordinary man in reaching into the lives of others. I had already spent years visiting hundreds of homes in the usual unannounced thirty minute way with very dismaying results.

For the next four or five years the material you will find here began to come together bit by bit. First, I tried one one-hour lesson, then one two-hour lesson. I later tried four lessons, but the final six-hour combination seemed to be what the Lord had in mind for me. It was all just material I carried around in my head for a long time. Then, in 1976, at the encouraging of a dear brother in the Lord, I put a rough copy of the material in writing.

Over the years I have worked to refine the material and make it clearer and easy to teach. All of the basic information remains the same. With this edition I have added a chapter to help you win a soul to Christ when you have only one opportunity. I have also made the chapter on training teachers the final chapter in the manual. Hopefully you will now find the material much easier to follow and teach. (In the lesson plan outlines, Scriptures to go on the chart are in bold type. All others are for your own reference in teaching).

And that's my goal, that multitudes will teach this material. These truths are not mine; they are the Lord's. He let me have the privilege of arranging them in the teaching order. I thank Him for that privilege and have tried to make it so easy that you will be able to simply take this material and go to work. May He make you fruitful as He has others who have already gotten into the work of presenting Christ to needy souls!

Lester Hutson

Explanatory Note

The material in this book is designed to be taught primarily in homes one hour per week for six weeks at an appointed time. Thus this is an evangelism and discipleship course. You will find the content along with advice on teaching and techniques in chapters one through six. Chapter seven tells you how to present Christ when you have only one brief opportunity. Chapter eight tells how to set up these lessons and discusses some very important teaching considerations. Chapter nine provides insight into the purpose of the course and explains how one may train himself or others to teach this material. This lesson sheds light on how to make the teaching of this course a working ministry of a Church.

What you have in your hands is thus a tool to be used, not just a book to be read. The material here is designed to equip you to go out and actually begin sharing the great truths of God's word with others. Before you go out, you should master the content of this book, not only the actual truths to be shared, but also the material on how to do it. First read the entire book with the idea of getting the whole concept in mind. Then begin to master the material so that you may share it with others effectively in the manner that is set forth here.

1
ONE

Looking at the World
Through the Eyes of God

> "*But the Lord said unto Samuel, Look not on his countenance, or on the height of his stature; because I have refused him: for the Lord seeth not as man seeth; for man looketh on the outward appearance, but the Lord looketh on the heart.*"
>
> 1 Samuel 16:7

TEACHER: HERE ARE YOUR OBJECTIVES FOR THIS LESSON

1. This first lesson will set the tone for the classes. You should attempt to establish an atmosphere of learning and favor toward the truths to be presented. Your first objective is to create a friendly and relaxed atmosphere. Your student will almost always be a little apprehensive as you begin these studies. Quite often someone religious has previously tried to ram something *down his throat.* He suspects that you will attempt the same. So, in almost

every case, his guard will be up to some degree. It is imperative that you put his fears and reservations at ease in this first lesson, not so much by verbal assurances as by your manner and approach.

Do not seek, in this lesson or the others, to bring about conviction in your student through your finesse, great knowledge of the Bible, pressuring for *a decision* or by some other energy of the flesh tactic. Such activity not only produces empty professions (when there is a profession at all), it also greatly undermines the confidence of the student in you and in what you are doing. The true success of your whole effort can be negated right here. Never forget that true conviction which leads to genuine decisions (by both the lost to receive Christ and the believer to true commitment to the Lordship of Christ) is wrought by the Holy Spirit through the Word of truth. The Word, which Hebrews 4:12 declares to be both quick (alive) and powerful, will do the job when presented faithfully in love. *"Faith cometh by hearing, and hearing by the word of God,"* Romans 10:17. Mark 16:15 makes clear that your assignment is to make sure men hear. Paul referred to this in 1 Corinthians 3:6-7 as planting and cultivating the spiritual seed however in the final analysis it is God who gives the increase. Anything short of that is, in God's opinion, no more than *"wood, hay, and stubble,"* 1 Corinthians 3:11-15.

To establish this atmosphere in which your student will trust you sufficiently to lower his guard to the point of really listening to what you have to say, be kind and gracious. Do not *push* your student. Let him follow you voluntarily. The minute you enter the house be friendly. Express a real interest in your student. Visit three or four minutes, but do not sit down except at the table where the lesson is to be taught. Once you've suggested that you get to the table to begin the lesson, assure your student that there will be no pressure. Let him know that you will not attempt to force him into any decision. You will point out to him that he may indeed need to make many decisions, but assure him any decision he makes will be his own with no duress or pressure from you. Assure him that your mission is simply to share with him in a systematic, orderly way truths which you've seen and which have become precious and revolutionary to your own life. Perhaps as you share, your student will want to make these truths his own, but he will find himself under no obligation or pressure from you to do so.

Once you've made that promise live up to your promise. As your student opens his ears to listen teach him these truths in the most excellent, efficient, loving and zealous manner possible. Do all within your power to help him to see. Be compassionate and patient and you will no doubt be joyously amazed as you watch the Spirit of God work through His Word.

2. The actual teaching objective of lesson one is to bring your student, who may or may not have confidence in the Bible, to a belief that the Bible really is God's Word, and that the only sure way to know what God thinks is through His Word. To achieve this primary objective the following secondary objectives should be pursued in the order listed:

   a. See that your student understands these to be fundamental or basic truths of the Christian faith.

   b. Help your student see that a primary objective of these lessons is to look at the points under consideration from God's, not men's, point of view.

   c. See that your student realizes that it is only possible to get God's point of view by considering His book, the Bible.

   d. Make sure your student understands that if we limit our positions to those set forth in the Bible, our positions become truth, not mere religious denominational conjecture.

   e. See that your student realizes that from an eternal standpoint it is imperative to consider Bible truth while there is still time.

   f. Conclude this lesson by pointing out to your student that God has divided the whole human race into two basic divisions.

This is the simple approach for presenting lesson one. Depending upon the background of the student the delivery and emphasis of the lesson may vary considerably (as is true in each of the six lessons), but each of these points and objectives should be established.

PRESENTING

LESSON ONE

TEACHER: To insure your success in teaching this material you should learn the titles, thoughts and applications of each lesson. Do not merely memorize to *parrot* this book. Get this material into your heart so that you can put it in your own words. This information is being included at the beginning of each lesson in this *Teacher's Manual* to help you.

TITLE

"Looking at the World Through the Eyes of God"

THOUGHT

THE ONLY WAY TO LOOK ACCURATELY AT ANY THING IS TO LOOK AT IT FROM GOD'S VIEWPOINT WHICH IS ONLY POSSIBLE THROUGH THE BIBLE.

APPLICATION

To bring the student face to face with the reality of God's superior knowledge and the realization that no mortal can be sure of truth and reality apart from God's revelation. The Bible is God's revelation. As long as any man is true to the Bible, he can be sure he is right.

PRESENTING

Once you are seated at the table, the actual teaching should begin in earnest. Although the material is flexible and should be adapted to meet specific situations, here is the basic order I follow. In each case I shall attempt to give you the point at hand, the appropriate Scriptures and an appropriate illustration. Ultimately each teacher should choose the Scripture(s) with which he feels most adequate and develop his own set of illustrations.

Remember to start with a reassurance of the non-pressured approach you will use in teaching.

1. Consult the section explaining the first objective of this lesson.

2. Be sure and do this even though you have already done so when you set up the lessons.

Section One

Begin by making the point that this course is designed to cover primarily the fundamentals or basics of the Christian faith.

A. How to achieve the objective.

1. Explain that you are making no attempt to teach the whole Bible. It is far too big and broad for six one-hour lessons. Admit that you do not claim to be capable of teaching the whole Bible. No one knows all there is to know about the Bible. However explain that there are some things you do know and these are the things you are going to teach.

2. Explain that what you plan to teach will constitute the basics or fundamentals of the Christian faith.

B. *ILLUSTRATE HERE.*

Even as the foundation and framework of a house do not constitute a whole house, likewise these lessons do not constitute the whole of Christianity. These six lessons equate to the framework of a house. When a house is framed much work remains before completion however at that point the overall shape and pattern of the house is established. Likewise, once the truths of these lessons are understood a great frame of reference for all other Bible truths is set.

C. Next explain to your student that this course not only sets forth the fundamentals of Christianity, it also arranges these truths so as to establish a proper order which will present the big picture of Christianity.

    1. Explain that many people have much general knowledge of Christianity but that knowledge is in a jumbled order.

        a. They know Christianity involves faith and works, God and the devil, heaven and hell, baptism, church membership and good works. Yet they have little understanding of how these pieces fit; thus there's no grasp of the true picture of Christianity.

        b. This course will arrange these individual pieces or truths in proper order to show the big picture.

    2. *ILLUSTRATE HERE.*

    Build on the house illustration. Point out that a lot with every item necessary to the formation of a complete house on it does not necessarily constitute a house. To have a house the building materials must be properly arranged and connected. That's what these lessons will attempt to do with these fundamental or basic Bible truths.

D. This is a good place to mention:

    1. That each point will build upon the previous points. The material is ordered and structured.

    2. That questions should be kept primarily to the material of the course.

        a. Invite your student to ask questions as the lessons progress, but to limit them to the material at hand. Explain that you will not have time to deal with non-related questions, but that you will answer them at the end of the course, if necessary.

        b. Also explain that many questions will automatically be answered as the lessons develop. Explain that when you know the answer is coming, you will ask your student to wait briefly until your explanation is given.

6

3. That a chart will be developed. Briefly explain the chart and ask your student to keep up with it from week to week. Explain that you will build on it weekly.

Section Two

Explain now to your student that throughout these lessons a primary objective will be to look at all the points considered as God looks at them. Make the point that God views things very differently than men.

A. At this point write **God** at the top of the chart sheet and add **1 Samuel 16:7**. *(See chart #1)*

B. How to establish this point.

1. Point out that among men there are about as many opinions about spiritual points as there are men. What real reason is there to think one man's opinion is substantially better than any other's? Time passes and opinions change.

2. God too has an opinion on spiritual points but His opinion never changes. Time has repeatedly proven God to be always right whereas men have been wrong again and again. So, tell your student that the objective here is not to swap opinions or teach human concepts. The objective here is to learn God's opinion on each issue.

3. Explain that God's opinion is far superior to man's. Add **Isaiah 55:8-9** and read it. Because of His superior basis of judgment it is His opinion that really counts. Whereas men form their opinions mainly upon the basis of what they see and hear, God knows the heart. He knows everything that has ever been, all that is and all that shall ever be. He never forms an opinion based on what He sees and hears. What He sees and hears (which is everything) merely confirms what God already knew to be true. Teacher, at this point refer to 1 Samuel 16:7. It states that God looks on the heart while man looks on the outward appearance.

C. *ILLUSTRATE HERE.*

The context of 1 Samuel 16:7 is dealing with the anointing of David to be the future king of Israel. Knowing the basis of human judgment to be the outward appearance, God warned Samuel, who was to do the anointing, not to make the decision as to who to anoint. God instructed Samuel that He (God) would tell him who to anoint. When Samuel arrived in Bethlehem at Jesse's house he stated that he had come to anoint one of Jesse's sons to be the future king. Jesse didn't even bring forth his youngest son, David, for consideration. This is a vivid illustration of the weakness and unreliable nature of human judgment. Even a dad didn't know how to properly judge his own sons. As Samuel went down the row of Jesse's seven oldest sons God refused all of them. Each outwardly looked far more like future king material than David. However when David was eventually summonsed to the scene God instructed Samuel to anoint him.

Several months passed and Israel found herself at war with the Philistines. The three older brothers of David, who looked outwardly so much like kingly material, were drafted into King Saul's army; but when a face-off with the enemy came, particularly Goliath, these three men, along with all of Saul's army, fled in retreat and fear. (See 1 Samuel 17:24 at this point.) When David (just a lad) came to the battle site and perceived what was happening he sought permission from Saul to fight. He single-handedly ran toward Goliath and slew him. (See 1 Samuel 17:48-50.) He went on to become by far the greatest Israeli general and king of all time. In fact, he is the greatest among all of history's generals, kings, and leaders, Jew or Gentile. What men saw in David on the battlefield surprised everyone! Except God! With His superior knowledge and judgment God already knew the truth about David long before Goliath. He was looking on the heart while others were looking on the outward appearance. God always sees the heart. He is never fooled by outward appearances.

After the illustration, point out that all of us are still forming opinions daily just like Jesse did. We decide whether a person is good or bad, saved or lost, going to heaven or hell based on what we see and hear (the outward appearance). I often point out that should we be given the task of dividing ten people into

8

two groups, the lost and the saved, we'd do it based solely upon what we know of them: what claims they make, their track records, their answers to our questions, etc. Should Jesus suddenly show up He'd doubtless tell us that some of those we rated saved were not and some we judge to be lost were really saved. His judgment would not at all be on the basis of outward appearance or conduct. His judgment would be based upon the true condition of their hearts and their personal relationships (or lack of it) to Him.

If your student thinks this judgment discussion is a non-related point to current real life, remind him that all of us routinely do it. For example, suggest to your student that should you ask him to write down ten names of people he knows (some for many years and others he's just met), he could easily rate them as to the ones he thinks are saved and the ones who aren't. In fact, he has already subconsciously done so with all the people he knows. Furthermore, he did so upon the basis of what he saw and heard; their outward appearance.

God has done the same but not on the basis of outward conduct. He has already determined the spiritual condition of every man based upon the true condition of the heart.

Section Three

Next, teach your student that we do not know all things and see hearts as God does. The only way we can be sure our opinions are God's opinions and thus right opinions is by aligning our thinking and opinions with His expressed thinking and opinions. The Bible is where He has expressed His thinking and opinions.

A. How to teach this point.

    1. Tell your student that we claim that the Bible is God's Word, His thinking. However admit to him that many people do not believe it is. Thus, the questions, "Is it, and how do we know it is?" Acknowledge to him that the case of Christianity really rises and falls on the integrity of the Bible. If the Bible is not God's Word, then Christianity is nothing more than glorified human thinking. It is bankrupt. If the Bible is God's word, then our top priority should be to know what it says. We should then think accordingly.

2. With this groundwork established tell your student that there are ways to prove the Bible to be the Word of God. Tell him that you are now going to look briefly at three of those ways.

TEACHER: As you develop these proofs of the Bible you should begin adding the related points to the upper right hand corner of the chart, writing each point as you verbally establish the point. *(See the chart.)*

a. The first major proof that the Bible is God's Word is its **construction** or the way it came to be the book of perfect harmony that it is. Tell your student that he can check out the fact that the Bible is sixty-six separate books in one, each book having its own theme, plot and complete development. Yet it is a single book with a single theme (Jesus Christ) and a single plot (Christ's redemptive work for fallen man). In spite of the tremendous scope of its subject matter and all its types, foreshadowing and symbolism, it is amazingly a book of perfect harmony. Though many have tried, not one person has ever found even one error in it. Couple that fact with the realization that the Bible was written over sixteen centuries by more than forty men most of whom wrote separately from and without knowledge of each other. They were separated by generations and without intent of collaboration. One must admit that only God could have engineered and directed the project which we call the Bible. It is absolutely impossible that it could have come to exist otherwise.

b. The second major proof that the Bible is the thinking and work of God and not man is its **prophecies**. About two-thirds of the Bible is prophetic. Hundreds of Bible prophecies have already been fulfilled. Their fulfillment has been occurring for almost 4,000 years and so far the Bible has a 100% accuracy record. There is no way those writers could have known the people and events that would occur hundreds of years after their deaths. Yet they wrote of them with 100% accuracy. It is impossible to account for such phenomena except that God authored the Bible. He simply directed the writers in what to say.

TEACHER: It is good to point out a few specific prophecies and their fulfillments. Be careful that you do not bog down and spend too much of your time doing so. I recommend that you stay with simple, clear-cut prophecies and that you use no more than two. Here are suggestions:

When Joseph was a teenager God showed him that his brothers would bow down to him, Genesis 37:6-8. Years later when Joseph became Prime Minister of Egypt, it happened, Genesis 42:6.

In approximately 713 BC, Isaiah predicted that the Persian king, Cyrus, would issue an edict for Jerusalem to be rebuilt, Isaiah 44:28. History records that almost 200 years later Cyrus issued that proclamation, 2 Chronicles 36:23. It is noteworthy that at the time of Isaiah's prophecy Persia was not a ruling world power and Cyrus was not yet born.

c.   The third major proof of the Bible is its **claims** to be God's Word.

TEACHER: At this point I usually quote or read a few of the claims, listing them on the sheet as I do. Those I've found to be most effective are, in this order, **2 Peter 1:21, 2 Timothy 3:16,** and **1 Corinthians 2:9-10.** The key words are *"inspiration"* and *"revealed."* You can show from 1 Corinthians 2:9-10 that the Bible did not come about through (1) the scientific method of observation, (2) the general opinion or public consensus method or (3) the introspection or logic method. God *"revealed"* the information of the Bible (His own thinking) to men who merely recorded it as He directed. This explains its perfect harmony and accuracy.

11

B. Now make this point.

If the Bible is God's word (and the evidence says it is), then once we line up our thinking with the thinking of the Bible our positions and opinions become the positions and opinions of God. They are no longer merely the positions and doctrine of the Baptists, the Catholics or some other religious group. They are the positions of God.

TEACHER: This is a very important point to establish. Do not fail to make it clear.

Section Four

It is now time to tell your student that some people do not think that what God says or thinks about spiritual and eternal things really matters. Assure him that if the Bible is true (we've just seen that it is), then what God thinks is more important than anything.

A. As you teach this point fill in the appropriate information on the upper left hand corner of the chart.

B. How to establish this point.

Tell your student that, according to the Bible, everyone will ultimately give account of himself to God in a face-to-face judgment. The basis of that judgment will be the opinions or truths of God, not men. **Romans 14:11-12** predicts the judgment of God for every person, **Romans 2:2** says it will be according to truth and **John 17:17** says the Word of God is truth.

TEACHER: You should either quote or quickly turn to these passages to establish these points as you enter them on the chart.

C. *ILLUSTRATE HERE.*

When I was in school I knew tests were a certainty. The announcement of a test was no big, unexpected news. If the teacher gave the questions in advance, my odds for success were greatly enhanced. If my teacher had also given the correct answers in advance, there'd have been no legitimate reason for failure.

Basically, that is what God has done for all men. He has announced there is going to be a judgment or test for every man. He has given both the questions and correct answers in His book, the Bible. He has said no other answers will pass. The only thing He hasn't said is just when the test will be. Point out to your student that there is really no reason why any man should be unprepared and fail God's judgment. Stress again why it is so critically important to take a careful look at the basic or fundamental truths which God has set forth in the Bible.

Section Five

Tell your student that you will now conclude this first lesson by pointing out the fact that in God's opinion there are only two basic groups of people in the world.

A. As you teach this point draw the vertical line starting at the top with God downward to the bottom of your sheet. See the chart. As you talk add the words **No Relationship** and **Relationship** and add **Lost** and **Saved** as shown on the sample chart.

B. How to teach this part.

Tell your student that as the next lesson will fully show, God views the world's lost people as those who have no spiritual relationship with Him as contrasted to those who are saved because of their spiritual relationship with Him. Those not spiritually related to Him He defines as the *"lost."* Those spiritually related to Him He defines as the *"saved."* Tell your student that in the next lesson you will present a full look from God's viewpoint into each of these two divisions of people. At this point tell your student that this concludes lesson one.

AS YOU LEAVE:

1. Ask your student to keep up with the chart, and have it for next week's lesson. Explain that it can be a handy review sheet and that you'll add to it each week. Use of the same chart will prevent the delay of having to start from scratch each time.

2. Remind your student that you'll be back at the same time next week to teach lesson two which is titled *"The Hopelessness of a Wrong Relationship with God."*

3. Invite him to church.

4. Rise up and begin making your way to the door with a friendly goodbye.

Lesson One

Rom. 14:11,12
Rom. 2:2
John 17:17

1. Construction
2. Prophecies
3. Bible Claims
   2 Pet. 1:21
   2 Tim. 3:16
   1 Cor. 2:9,10

"NO RELATIONSHIP"
1. Lost

"RELATIONSHIP"
1. Saved

STUDY SHEET & LESSON PLAN

LESSON ONE

TITLE

"Looking at the World Through the Eyes of God"

THOUGHT

THE ONLY WAY TO LOOK ACCURATELY AT ANY THING
IS TO LOOK AT IT FROM GOD'S VIEWPOINT WHICH IS
ONLY POSSIBLE THROUGH THE BIBLE.

APPLICATION

To bring the student face to face with the reality of God's superior
knowledge and the realization that no mortal can be sure of truth and
reality apart from God's revelation. The Bible is God's revelation. As
long as any man is true to the Bible, he can be sure he is right.

BIBLE VERSES TO MEMORIZE

1 Samuel 16:7 *"But the Lord said unto Samuel, Look not on his countenance,
or on the height of his stature; because I have refused him: for the Lord seeth not
as man seeth; for man looketh on the outward appearance but the Lord looketh
on the heart."*

1 Corinthians 2:9-10 *"But as it is written, Eye hath not seen, nor ear heard,
neither have entered into the heart of man, the things which God hath prepared
for them that love him. But God hath revealed them unto us by His Spirit: for
the Spirit searcheth all things, yea, the deep things of God."*

Romans 14:11-12 *"For it is written, As I live, saith the Lord, every knee shall bow to me, and every tongue shall confess to God. So then every one of us shall give account of himself to God."*

Romans 2:2 *"But we are sure that the judgment of God is according to truth against them which commit such things."*

John 17:17 *"Sanctify them through thy truth: thy word is truth."*

OUTLINE

LESSON ONE

I. **Setting many fundamental or basic Bible truths in order.**

    A. No attempt to teach the whole Bible, only the basics.
ILLUSTRATE HERE: Framework to a house; it won't tell all, but it will tell much.

    B. Basic truths will be arranged in a systematic order.

        1. *ILLUSTRATE HERE:* To form a house building materials must be properly arranged.

        2. *TRANSITION THOUGHT:* A systematic approach.

II. **All lessons will attempt to look at things the way GOD does.**

    A. Many opinions among men and they change, but God's opinions never change.

    B. His basis of consideration is different and far superior to man's. **1 Samuel 16:7** and **Isaiah 55:8-9**

    ILLUSTRATE HERE: The anointing and performance of King David. The trend among men continues.

    TRANSITION THOUGHT: God's opinion is based upon the true condition of the heart.

III. **Knowledge of what God thinks is possible only through the Bible.**

    A. How we know the Bible is God's Word.

        1. **Construction**

        2. **Prophecies**

        3. **Claims: 2 Peter 1:21; 2 Timothy 3:16; 1 Corinthians 2:9-10.**

    B. If we stay with the positions of the Bible, our positions become the positions of God.

    TRANSITION THOUGHT: Not Baptist or denominational thinking, but God's truth.

IV. **What God thinks does matter.**

    A. Every man shall face Him in judgment. **Romans 14:11-12.**

    B. His judgment will be according to His Word of truth. **Romans 2:2.**

    C. The Bible is His Word of truth. **John 17:17.**

    ILLUSTRATION: A pre-announced test in school.

    TRANSITION THOUGHT: The importance of taking a careful look at what God thinks.

V. **God has divided the world into two basic divisions.**

    A. No relationship. LOST

    B. Relationship. SAVED

CONCLUDING THOUGHT: You will explain these in detail in the next lesson. The title of that lesson is ***"The Hopelessness of a Wrong Relationship with God."***

19

2

TWO

The Hopelessness of a Wrong Relationship with God

> *"In this the children of God are manifest, and the children of the devil: whosoever doeth not righteousness is not of God, neither he that loveth not his brother."*
>
> 1 John 3:10

TEACHER: **HERE ARE YOUR OBJECTIVES FOR THIS LESSON**

1. Your first objective is to see that your student grasps the concept that there is a sharp difference and contrast between those who are God's children and those who are not. As you develop your case which establishes this position emphasize that this difference and contrast is not readily apparent to human observation.

2. Your second objective is to establish in your student's mind the reality of the awful future eternal damnation of all who are not God's children.

3. Your third objective is to prove biblically that it is impossible for anyone to change his own relationship to God.

4. Your final objective in this lesson is to show that apart from divine intervention a wrong relationship with God is a hopeless condition in which to exist.

PRESENTING

LESSON TWO

TEACHER: Again be reminded of the importance of learning this title, thought and application. Learn it; don't just parrot it. Make sure you understand these truths so that you can explain them in your own words.

TITLE

"The Hopelessness of a Wrong Relationship with God"

THOUGHT

THOSE WHO HAVE NO RELATIONSHIP WITH GOD ARE IN AN ETERNALLY DISASTROUS CONDITION FROM WHICH THEY CANNOT SAVE THEMSELVES.

APPLICATION

To bring the student to an understanding of the fact that conduct is not the basis upon which God divides the world into two divisions. Also, to show from God's Word that those who have no relationship with God are powerless to bring themselves into a relationship with Him.

PRESENTING

Remember to always approach the home and conduct yourself therein with respect. Be cordial and in a relaxed, at-ease spirit. This sets a tone and atmosphere of reception, openness and learning with your student which is very important to the success of the endeavor although you should never take things for granted. Don't become too familiar with your student. Practice respect. You are the invited guest. Work to keep the atmosphere cordial, favorable and positive.

After a brief greeting, move right to the teaching table. You should never sit down until you get to the table, and your initial greetings should not involve more than three to five minutes. Your student knows you are coming to teach and is expecting you to do it. The opening greetings should consist of warm and sincere questions about him and his life since last week's meeting. A brief discussion of other matters might surface, but failure to get to the table to begin lesson two will eat into your one hour of time to teach lesson two and cause you to violate your time promise.

Once seated at the teaching table spread the chart which your student has kept. Put your Bible (and his) on the table. Begin with a little time reviewing last week's lesson. This is very important! It refreshes the student's memory of the last lesson and it enables you to link or tie into it with a natural and smooth progression. Your student will hardly know that you are reviewing or when you finish reviewing and proceed with new material. You should work at making this a natural and easy part of your teaching.

I suggest that you start your review with a reminder that in all of these studies our objective is to look at things the way God does and that the only legitimate way we have to do that is through the Bible. Remind your student that you have already given attention to proofs that the Bible is God's inspired book. In view of the fact that it is you are going to stay with the Bible in these studies thus establishing Bible positions, not just religious positions. Remind your student that according to the Bible God has divided all mankind into two basic divisions or groups.

Section One

You are now ready to spend time showing how God compares and contrasts the two basic groups.

A. How to develop and teach these comparisons and contrasts.

    1. I personally find it much more natural and effective to run the two columns point by point examining both sides of the issue as I go. For example, I fully compare and contrast being lost with being saved (the first entries in each column) before moving to a comparison and contrast of condemnation and justification (the second entries in each column). Fully developing the first column before addressing the second column requires the student to retain what you said about the items of column one until you get back to the corresponding point in column two. The retention span of the average student will be overtaxed. This will force you to repeat what you already said and thus waste valuable time.

2. On the chart I have listed only six comparisons and contrasts. There are dozens of others however these are adequate to establish the point that the salvation of God is by grace, not works. Teachers are always subject to overkill. Once to point is made move on lest you bog down. It is easy to use so much of your time fortifying a point that is already established that you do not have adequate time to make a later point of equal importance. You must balance your time and keep moving. Your objective is to present the big, overall picture. Too much time on any area of the material will not allow you to accomplish that in the six allotted hours.

I have chosen six key comparisons and contrasts which I consider to be generally adequate to establish the first objective of this lesson. Depending upon the background and condition of your student you may need to use different or more comparisons and contrasts. I also recommend presenting them in the order shown here. This sequence builds the case in a systematic way. The inherent logic builds a powerful case.

B. First compare and contrast being lost with being saved.

1. At the end of the first lesson you wrote *Lost* in the *No Relationship* column and *Saved* in the *Relationship* column. Now add **Luke 19:10** beside *Lost* and **Ephesians 2:8-9** beside *Saved* as shown on the chart.

2. Explain that this is God's terminology as stated right in the Bible. All of the comparisons and contrasts will be taken directly from Scripture.

3. *TEACHER:* I do not spend much time elaborating on this first comparison and contrast because with each new comparison and contrast the realization of what it means to be lost as opposed to what it means to be saved will emerge ever clearer.

C. Second compare and contrast *condemned* with *justified.*

1. As you write **Condemned** in the appropriate column explain that those who have no relationship with God are condemned. Explain that *condemned* is a legal term. When people break the law and are found guilty they are *condemned* by the law. Add **John 3:18** beside *Condemned* and quote or read it.

ILLUSTRATE HERE.

If I drive 50 miles per hour through a 15 mile per hour school zone, I have violated the law of the land. If a peace officer catches me doing so, he writes me a citation and may haul me to jail. In such a case I am *condemned* by the law. In a spiritual sense every person has violated God's law and God has caught each one. Thus every transgressor has been condemned by God's law. Every sinner, who has no relationship with God, is in that condition.

2. Next explain that all saved persons have a spiritual relationship to God and are *justified.* Write **Justified** in column two. Explain that *justified* is also a legal term. People who have no offence against the law are in a just position with the law. Write **Romans 5:1**.

ILLUSTRATE HERE.

Consider again driving 50 miles per hour through a school zone. I am apprehended by the peace officer, tried and found guilty. I am condemned to a $200 fine or thirty days in jail. I do not have the money so I'm off to jail. But, suppose someone volunteers to pay my fine for me. I agree to accept his payment on my behalf. He pays my fine and I go free. I am now *justified* with the law. Once my penalty is paid, I am *just* with the law. The law no longer has an offence against me. It is not that I never broke the law and am not guilty. No sir! I did it. I did break the law, but somebody paid my penalty, so I'm *justified* in the eyes of the law.

25

Explain to your student that being *justified* before God does not mean that a person never did wrong. To the contrary, all the people who are saved and in relationship to God have done wrong, many times! But, something marvelous has happened. As we shall see more clearly in future lessons God has paid the penalty for all of those who have a spiritual relationship with Him. They have accepted His payment on their behalf and by His own laws of divine justice He considers them *"justified."*

TEACHER: **EMPHASIZE** that guilt or innocence is not the issue in whether or not a person is *justified* or *condemned.* The issue is whether or not the guilt has been properly addressed. With the lost, it hasn't; with the saved, it has. One of the main things you must communicate in these lessons is the fact that God has not divided mankind into these two groups upon the basis of conduct, good or bad. You must show them that the basis of His dividing is whether or not their sin issue has been addressed. Sin cannot be addressed by what man can do for his self. Man's sin can be adequately addressed by God. You must hammer and hammer at this truth, even as the Bible does. Basically ingrained into every man is the idea that people are saved because their conduct is better than the conduct of lost people and that people are lost because their conduct isn't good enough. Most religions teach that. Many "Christian" denominations make this false claim. You must systematically destroy that false concept with the Word of God as you move through this course. One explanation by you won't do it. You must keep hammering at it with the Word, not too abruptly at first lest you alienate your student. Keep staying with it letting the Word do the hammering with one passage after another until the student sees it for himself, not from you but from God's Word. This second lesson should drive the spike really deep into the heart of the false *works* or *good conduct for salvation* concept. You have to convince your student from the Word that God's basis of salvation is not *works* or *good or bad conduct.* It is rather faith in Jesus Christ based on His work on the cross for sinners. Teacher, you are laying the basic groundwork for that concept right here at this section of lesson two.

D. Next compare and contrast *un-forgiven* with *forgiven*.

1. Explain that those who have no relationship with God are in that condition because they are *un-forgiven*. As you are saying this write **Un-forgiven** in column one and add **Acts 13:38-39**. This is a profound, yet easy to establish point. It builds naturally upon the points you've just made. Here you can point out the observable reality that all men are sinners. You might quote a passage like Romans 3:23 or Ecclesiastes 7:20. Point out that those in the *No Relationship* column are no more sinners than those in the *Relationship* column. Those in the *No Relationship* column are there simply and only because they have not been forgiven. Their conduct may be worse or better than those in the *Relationship* column but conduct (good or bad) has nothing to do with why they're *lost* and in the *No Relationship* column. They remain *lost* only because they are *un-forgiven*.

2. In *the Relationship* column write **Forgiven** and add **Ephesians 1:7**. Again the point to establish is that those in this column are there simply and only because they've been forgiven, not because they are sin-free or because they committed only a small number of sins. The idea that should ever grow as you teach these points is that conduct, good or bad, is not God's basis for placement of men into one group or the other.

   ILLUSTRATE HERE.

   At this point I often tell my student of a common bumper sticker I've seen. It simply says, *"Christians aren't perfect; just forgiven."* That's true but it's a concept few seem to grasp.

E. Your fourth entry should be a comparison and contrast between *unrighteous* and *righteous*.

1. In teaching this point, first write **Unrighteous** in column one and place **Romans 1:18** beside it. Explain that to be unrighteous is to not be righteous. Remind your student that we are thinking here in terms of those whom God considers righteous, not necessarily those whom men consider righteous. Literally, an *unrighteous* person is one whom God considers not right with Him.

2. On the other hand those in column two are *righteous* or those whom God considers right with Him. Write **Righteous** in column two and add **Romans 3:22**.

TEACHER: At this point in teaching this comparison and contrast you have an excellent opportunity to make a tremendously powerful point. Don't miss it. Explain from **Romans 3:22** (turn there and read or quote it) that God's *"righteousness"* is available to everyone (*"unto all"*), but it is the actual possession (*"upon all"*) of only those who believe.

ILLUSTRATE HERE.

If on a certain day between 9:00 and noon a local grocery store offered ten pounds of choice T-bone steaks to every customer, some would take advantage of the free offer and some wouldn't. Though the offer be "unto all," it would only be "upon all" those who take advantage of it. For all others it may as well never have been offered. Those who didn't respond may have failed to do so for a variety of reasons, but the bottom line would always be the same. The offer would profit them nothing, though it could have. Some might refuse to respond to the offer out of downright disbelief of its legitimacy and others for skepticism of a hidden danger. Still others might intend to respond but be side-tracked by some other matter. A few would be discouraged by the long waiting line. Doubtless many would intend to take advantage but fail due to neglect. In each case the bottom line would be the same: no steaks.

Likewise, God has offered to make all men righteous or right with Him. His only limit is a time limit; the offer must be accepted during one's mortal lifetime. Some have come to Him and have been made righteous, yet others haven't. Some of those who haven't just don't believe *this God and Bible stuff.* Others accept the facts, but have never gotten around to taking advantage of God's offer. They intend to do so but are still in neglect. Still others haven't come because of the hypocrites. Many are too busy, consumed with other matters. But, whatever the reason the bottom line is the same: they are all still *unrighteous.* Romans 3:22 says God's righteousness is available *"unto all"* of them, but it is only *"upon all"* those who have believed in Jesus Christ as personal Savior. But, the question is, what is this *"righteousness of God"* which is the possession of some but which others don't have? One this is obviously certain; it is *"the righteousness of God,"* not man. So those in column two who are said to be *righteous* are not *righteous* because they do more right deeds than those in column one. Romans 1:16-17 says this *"righteousness of God"* which could be the personal possession of every man is a part of the *"gospel of Christ."* The gospel of Christ is defined as Christ's death, burial and resurrection, 1 Corinthians 15:1-4. The righteous act of God in the gospel is the fact that He paid the sinner's penalty by His own death on the cross. When He died there He was doing it for sinners, 1 Peter 2:24. In view of the fact that the penalty for sin is death, Romans 6:23, there is no other way sinners can be forgiven and given eternal life short of the Savior's death on their behalf. God, knowing that to be true, came in the person of Jesus Christ and went to the cross in the stead of sinners, Romans 5:6,8. In the history of the world many right things have been done, but none can compare with the right act of God on the cross in dying for sinners. It was and is the one and only hope for fallen men.

This righteous act of God is now offered to the credit of every man. In simple terms God credits His death on the cross to every person who believes on Christ. Turn your student to Romans 4:1-6 and let him see it for himself. The text is discussing how Abraham (and all men) was justified before God (verse 2). Verses 4 and 5 say it was definitely not by works (conduct). Verses 3, 5 and 6 say God's righteousness is *"counted"* (our word is *accounted* as in an accountant's terminology) or *"imputed"* (given without merit or charge) to everyone who believes. Isn't that great! God just gives His (God's) own righteousness to every sinner who comes to Christ. On the eternal ledger-book of God the death of Jesus Christ is credited to every sinner who believes. God looks at that sinner just as though he died on the cross for he did in the person of Christ by identification through faith. Christ died for that sinner, paid that sinner's death penalty. As God legally sees it that sinner is *righteous* or right with Him. But notice, that sinner is not righteous upon the strength of what he did for himself through better conduct; he is reckoned *righteous* by God upon the strength of what God did for him.

ILLUSTRATE HERE.

Say to your student something like this: Suppose someone came to you and said *"I want to give you a large sum of money."* You've never worked for that person or done anything to merit one cent from him. He owes you nothing. But, you go with him to the bank where a new account is opened exclusively in your name. Then the new accounts secretary asks how much you wish to deposit in the account as you open it. The man speaks up and says, *"$100,000."* She asks, *"Check?"* He says, *"No; cash!"* Then he pulls out the biggest roll of bills you have ever seen and places $100,000 on the desk. The big boys in the back are called, but the money is not *hot*; it is all legitimate. The secretary then gives you a deposit slip for $100,000 and the stranger leaves. Suddenly you have $100,000 which only you can touch. You didn't inherit it, work for it or in any way deserve it. He just gave it to you freely; imputed it to your account.

TEACHER: Drive this truth home like a sledge to a spike. God has done something infinitely more dramatic and outstanding than give someone $100,000. He has given His death on the cross to every sinner who has come in faith to Him through Christ. All sinners who trust Christ are infinitely rich and have eternal life, but not because they've done any good thing. They're there because God put them there upon the strength of His work on their behalf. All men could be *righteous* but only believers are. The difference is not conduct, good or bad; the difference is in whether or not the righteousness of God has been imputed.

F. Then point out to your student that those who remain *unrighteous* are said to be *"dead in trespasses and sins"* while the *righteous* have *"eternal life."*

    1. Along with **Ephesians 2:1** write **Dead in trespasses and sins** in column one. Explain that to be *dead* means to be in a state of separation. When the spirit leaves the body, the coroner says the subject is dead. Of course, he is speaking of mortal or physical death. To be *"dead in trespasses and sins"* is to be in a state of spiritual separation from God. The subject may be very alive physically yet be in a position where he or she has no communications with, or grounds of contact, with God. This is the state in which Adam and Eve found themselves when they sinned against God in Eden. There could be no fellowship with God as long as they remained in that condition. Like all lost people are they were in a state of spiritual separation from God.

2. However, once people come in faith to Christ, they are given **Eternal life.** Add this to column two and write **John 5:24.** Emphasize that the life is called *"eternal."* This verse lends itself especially well to an emphasis of the eternal security of the believer. I always quote this verse while having my student follow me in his Bible. As I go through it I point to the various parts of the chart which are touched by this verse. I particularly emphasize the fact that once a person arrives in column two he cannot get back into condemnation. This verse says so directly.

G. Finally on my list of comparisons and contrasts, I list *eternity in the lake of fire* and *Heaven.*

1. At this point write **Eternity in the lake of fire** in column one and pair **Revelation 20:14-15** with it.

   TEACHER: You ought to spend time at this point talking about what an awful place a lake of fire is. I doubt that I need to spend much time here telling you how to establish this point.

2. On the other side of the dividing line add **Heaven** and put **John 14:1-3** beside it. Heaven is where God is and all believers are going there for eternity. They're going there, not because they've done good things and deserve to go there, but because they've been saved, justified, forgiven, made right with God and been given eternal life upon the strength of the work Jesus did on the cross.

31

TRANSITION THOUGHT.

When you get to the discussion of heaven, let this be a reminder to you that you are about to change direction to a second major thought.

Section Two

Make clear to your student that every person in group one is headed to the lake of fire.

A. **TEACHER:** You've already largely established this point with your sixth comparison and contrast however the point is so important that it really needed to be re-emphasized.

1. Be careful at this point. Do not make it appear that you are pointing your finger at your student and telling him he is going to hell. He may be lost and on his way to hell. If he is, most likely he has begun to see it by this point in the studies. If you are faithful to stay with the Scriptures, they will convict him to the core about his condition. Don't try to be the one who convicts him; let the Holy Spirit through the Word bring about the conviction.

2. I usually again quote or read Revelation 20:14-15 again at this point and point out what an awful thing it would be for anyone to mortally die while still in column one. Other good Scriptures to use are Psalm 9:17, 2 Thessalonians 1:7-9 and John 3:36. I always point out that sooner or later everyone in columns one and two must mortally die. It is up to every man to decide which side of the ledger he will be on when he dies. Whether he is lost or saved when he dies will not be determined by his conduct, bad or good, but by whether or not he by faith has taken advantage of what God has done for him in Christ.

B. This is a good place to remind your student of a point you made in lesson one.

1. Because we mortals look on the outward appearance we can't look at other people and tell whether or not they're headed to heaven or to the lake of fire. Our judgment of such a

matter would have to be made upon the basis of conduct which is not the true basis for such a judgment at all.

2. But God looks on the heart. He knows the true condition of every person. He knows which column is theirs and He's the one, who when mortal death comes, will see to it that the eternal spirit goes either to heaven or to the lake of fire. His call will be made upon the individual's relationship (or lack thereof) to God, not that individual's conduct. There is no escaping eternity in the lake of fire for those who remain in column one.

TEACHER: This is your transition thought.

Section Three

At this point make sure your student realizes that there is absolutely nothing any person in group one can possibly do for himself to change his condition and get into a proper relationship to God.

A. Tell your student that once most people recognize themselves to be in group one and headed to eternal fire they usually respond by attempting to substantially improve their conduct.

1. Go to the chart and draw **the horizontal line** below the *No Relationship* entries. At the left cut the horizontal line with a vertical line and write in **Love**. Point out that lost people know that love is a good and noble trait. They suppose that if they are ever going to make heaven they must love one another. Thus, in an effort to get into the second column many people attempt to add love to their lives. Most figure that's not enough, so they also add baptism. (Make a second vertical cut and add **Baptism**.) Who could be against being baptized? Your student knows that anyone really serious about being saved would want to be baptized. Furthermore, really serious ones will want to be an active part of a church. Many become members, attend faithfully and even work in a church actively. (Add a third vertical cut and write in **Church**.) Add a fourth vertical cut and write in **Worship**. Tell your student that to **Sing, Give, Pray, Preach** and observe the **Lord's Supper** are all acts of worship. Many

33

attempt these hoping to be saved thereby. Add these to the chart as you teach. The really serious ones work hard at it through great service. Add **Service** as shown. Talk about how many people try to be better as an employee, mate, parent, neighbor and citizen. They think that by good conduct they will surely make it to heaven.

2. **TEACHER:** It's time now for you to *draw the net* on the false *good conduct for salvation* concept. On the chart enter **the big horizontal parenthesis** as shown on your sample chart at the end of this chapter. Above it write **100% Good Conduct.** As you are doing this say to your student, *"Let's suppose we could find one person who practiced 100% good conduct."* This statement opens the door to a discussion along the following lines. Tell your student that you know and he knows there is nobody in that category. Romans 3:23 says there is not. But, just for hypothetical purposes, suppose there was one with 100% good conduct. Even if there was, he'd still be on the wrong side of the dividing line. He'd still be in the hell bound column because good conduct is not the basis for making the change from column one to column two. Nowhere in the Bible is there any hint that a person who does 51% good of his time and evil only 49% of his time will make heaven. Neither is there any indication that a 99% good to 1% evil ratio will get anyone saved. The Bible just doesn't deal in such human nonsense. What it does do is consistently insist that salvation is only possible upon the basis of God's work on the cross for sinners, not by any sort of human effort or conduct be it good or bad.

ILLUSTRATE HERE.

I often illustrate this point by telling my student that if I had the funds of a multi-billionaire, I could hire myself any number of people who would meticulously follow the spectrum of good conduct. If I could pay a person $1,000 a day, I could doubtless get plenty of the rankest, lost sinners to work for me with the job assignment of living like a *Christian.* For $1,000 a day they'd be glad to pay their tithes and still have $900 left. To keep a high paying job like that they'd attend every church service, pray often, sing in the choir, be baptized several times and go out of their way to love everybody and do good deeds.

However anyone with the slightest perception knows that running the good conduct spectrum for hire doesn't mean a person really is a Christian. For the person in the scenario above, it would all be just a job, *pretense* in order to get the money. The point is obvious. A brilliant display of good conduct is no certain indicator that a person is in a right relationship with God. A lost person can act more sanctimonious than a saved person but he is still lost and on his way to the lake of fire. God is looking at the true condition of the heart; not outward acts of conduct. If the heart has been made right by God's sacrificial provision, then the person is in group two. If the heart has not been made right by God's sacrificial provision, then regardless of the high level of good conduct which he may be performing, the person is in group one.

TEACHER: Remember what you are doing here. You are trying to get rid of the works and good conduct idea of salvation which is likely held by your student. Your goal is to get him to give up on his own abilities so he'll be in a mental position to look to and accept Jesus Christ, whom you will present as the answer to salvation in the next two lessons. So, here you are establishing essential groundwork, not only by biblically undermining the false self-salvation concept, but by suggesting repeatedly that the answer to salvation is in Jesus Christ.

ILLUSTRATE HERE AGAIN.

Since the teaching at this point has been dealing with add-on conduct and artificial acting of a role this illustration has proven especially enlightening.

I say to my student something like this: *"Just suppose I said to you, 'How would you like for me to plant a pecan tree in your yard?'"* You might say to me, *"Well Preacher, I'd like that. I've needed a good tree over in that right front corner for a long time."* So, I say *"Next week I'll come an hour or two early and plant the tree"* and you say *"Come on. I'll be here to tell you exactly where to plant it."*

35

Next week at the appointed time, I show up ready to plant the pecan tree, and say *"O.K. where do you want it?"* You say, *"Right here, Preacher."* I go to my truck and bring out the shovel, potting soil, root stimulator and everything I need to dig the hole and plant the tree. You stand there and watch while I dig the hole and get everything ready for the actual planting. Then I say, *"I'll be right back,"* and I go to my truck and return with a fine set of pecan tree roots. I saturate them with root stimulator and neatly arrange them in the hole. I say, *"You are really going to like this tree. It's a beauty and it's a great pecan; a really good variety. Wait just a minute; I'll be back with the trunk of the tree."* By then you're beginning to think I'm losing my mind and have gone off the deep end, but you watch. Sure enough, I return from my truck with the trunk of the tree which I have cut at a neat slant to fit the slant I made on the roots. I join the trunk to the roots and securely tape the two together, smooth the mixture of potting soil just right and pour in more root stimulator. Then, I say *"Just a minute, I'll get the limbs";* and to your disbelief, I return with a nice set of limbs and begin to tape and wire them in place on the trunk of the tree. I say, *"It's really shaping up, isn't it? It's going to be a nice tree. It's almost eight feet tall with nice long limbs. Let me get the leaves."* You watch in utter shock as I return with a sack of green pecan leaves and start clipping them in place all over the tree. Then I say, *"I didn't want to bring you a tree that wasn't producing, so I brought these pecans."* Sure enough, I start clipping pecans on the tree. Then I say, *"How do you like it?"* You try to be nice because we're friends, but you say, *"Preacher, I don't believe it's going to work."* I say, *"Why not? It has everything a pecan tree is supposed to have, and doesn't it look nice?"* But you say, *"Preacher, it does look nice outwardly, but that tree lacks the one most essential element, the main ingredient. It has no life."*

I then say to my student, *"You are exactly right. The tree lacks life. You don't build a tree by starting with all the outward, observable parts of the tree, putting them together hoping they'll generate life. No. Just the reverse is necessary if you are going to have a tree. You start with life, a seed or an already living tree. You plant it and then, in time, the outward symptoms follow: roots, a trunk, limbs, leaves and ultimately fruit."* I then explain to my student that this is exactly how it is with becoming a Christian, getting saved, getting into the family of God. So many people think they'll go to heaven if they put on the outward symptoms which they equate with being saved: loving, being baptized, going to church, worshipping and serving. Being good and making sure your good outweighs your bad is noble thinking but those things added to a person's life won't any more make him a saved person than adding roots, a trunk, limbs, leaves and pecans will make a pecan tree. They're all fine and dandy, but they don't produce life. Spiritually the exact reverse is necessary. As we shall see in a later lesson God says that in order to be saved one must start with life which comes with a new birth. Once a person has life he then is in relationship to God as shown in the second column. The good works and other symptoms of a Christian will come, not artificially, but spontaneously and naturally as the newborn Christian grows toward maturity.

TEACHER: Drive this truth home. The starting place is life, not the addition of more and better conduct.

B. You should now show your student that the Word of God confirms what you are saying.

1. As you quote or turn to these Scriptures begin writing them onto the chart in the area shown on the sample chart at the end of this lesson. I usually give the Scriptures in this order, briefly commenting and emphasizing the *No works* aspects of each one as I go: **Ephesians 2:8-9**, **Titus 3:5**, **Isaiah 64:6**, and **Romans 4:5**. I often point out that this is contrary to what you'll hear in a great many churches. Churches sometimes tend to imply that living better and faithfully performing religious activity will somehow result in salvation. God flatly says they won't. Remind your student that it is what God says that really counts. His Word is more important than my opinion, your opinion, the church's opinion, the Pope's opinion, mother's opinion or other opinion. He says a person absolutely does not go from group one to group two by his own efforts or conduct. If he is ever to get from group one to group two, it will be because God made it happen, not by what he did for himself.

2. At this point, mark the big **X** through the whole works or good conduct section as a visible symbol that this method will not work as a means of salvation. It cannot re-locate anyone in group one into group two.

    TEACHER: Here is where you conclude this lesson. You do so by pointing out that to be in group one is a hopeless condition. That does not mean a person in that group cannot be helped, rescued or saved from his hopeless condition. He can be rescued but he cannot rescue himself. The only hope for him is that someone else will do it for him. He is absolutely powerless to save himself. If he is ever to be saved, someone else will have to save him.

AS YOU LEAVE:

1. Tell your student that next week's lesson is titled *"What God Has Done for the Lost World."* Explain that this lesson will show how God is the one who can move a person from group one to group two.

2. Remind your student to keep up with the chart and that you'll add more to it next week.

3. Invite him to church.

4. Rise up and make your way to the door with a friendly goodbye.

Lesson Two

Rom. 14:11,12
Rom. 2:2
John 17:17

GOD
1 Sam. 16:7

1. Construction
2. Prophecies
3. Bible Claims
   2 Pet. 1:21
   2 Tim. 3:16
   1 Cor. 2:9,10

"NO RELATIONSHIP"
1. Lost
   Luke 19:10

2. **Condemned**
   John 3:18

3. **Unforgiven**
   Acts 13:38-39

4. **Unrighteous**
   Rom. 1:18

5. **Dead in trespasses**
   and sins
   Eph. 2:1

6. **Eternity in the**
   lake of fire
   Rev. 20:14-15

"RELATIONSHIP"
1. Saved
   Eph. 2:8-9

2. **Justified**
   Rom. 5:1

3. **Forgiven**
   Eph. 1:7

4. **Righteous**
   Rom. 3:22

5. **Eternal Life**
   John 5:24

6. **Heaven**
   John 14:1-3

100% GOOD CONDUCT

Love | Baptism | Church | Worship | Service

Eph. 2:8-9   **Isa. 64:6**
Titus 3:5   **Rom. 4:5**

1. Sing
2. Give
3. Pray
4. Preach
5. Lord's Supper

STUDY SHEET & LESSON PLAN
LESSON TWO

TITLE

"The Hopelessness of a Wrong Relationship with God"

THOUGHT

THOSE WHO HAVE NO RELATIONSHIP WITH GOD ARE
IN AN ETERNALLY DISASTROUS CONDITION FROM
WHICH THEY CANNOT SAVE THEMSELVES.

APPLICATION

To bring the student to an understanding of the fact that conduct is
not the basis upon which God divides the world into two divisions.
Also, to show from God's Word that those who have no relationship
with God are powerless to bring themselves into a relationship with
Him.

BIBLE VERSES TO MEMORIZE

Ephesians 2:8-9 *"For by grace are ye saved through faith; and that not of
yourselves: it is the gift of God: Not of works, lest any man should boast."*

Romans 3:21-22 *"But now the righteousness of God without the law is
manifested, being witnessed by the law and the prophets; Even the righteousness of
God which is by faith of Jesus Christ unto all and upon all them that believe: for
there is no difference."*

Romans 4:4-5 *"Now to him that worketh is the reward not reckoned of grace, but of debt. But to him that worketh not, but believeth on him that justifieth the ungodly, his faith is counted for righteousness."*

John 5:24 *"Verily, verily, I say unto you, He that heareth my word, and believeth on him that sent me, hath everlasting life, and shall not come into condemnation; but is passed from death unto life."*

Titus 3:5 *"Not by works of righteousness which we have done, but according to his mercy he saved us, by the washing of regeneration, and renewing of the Holy Ghost."*

OUTLINE

LESSON TWO

I. **How God compares and contrasts the two basic groups.**

    A. Compare and contrast being **lost, Luke 19:10,** with being **saved, Ephesians 2:8-9.**

    B. Compare and contrast being **condemned, John 3:18,** with being **justified, Romans 5:1.**

        1. *Condemned* and *justified* are legal terms.

        2. Condemnation illustration: speeding through a school zone.

        3. Justification illustration: someone pays my fine.

    C. Compare and contrast being **un-forgiven, Acts 13:38-39,** with being **forgiven, Ephesians 1:7.**

        1. Emphasize that the difference in the groups is not determined by guilt or innocence, but by forgiveness or un-forgiveness.

        2. *ILLUSTRATE HERE:* Bumper sticker - *"Christians aren't perfect, just forgiven."*

    D. Compare and contrast **unrighteous, Romans 1:18,** with **righteous, Romans 3:22.**

        1. Key: *Righteousness* in God's opinion is not established by the good deeds one does, but by the right act of God (Christ's death on the cross) credited to his spiritual account.

2. ***ILLUSTRATE HERE:*** Free offer of T-bone steaks by a local grocery store.

3. Explain that God's righteous act, which is available to sinners, was His death in their place on the cross. Scriptures to use in this order to establish the point: Romans 3:22, Romans 1:16-17, 1 Corinthians 15:1-4, 1 Peter 2:24, Romans 6:23, Romans 5:6-8 and Romans 4:1-6.

4. ***ILLUSTRATE HERE:*** A large sum of money given to you.

E. Compare and contrast **dead in trespasses and sins, Ephesians 2:1,** with **eternal life, John 5:24.**

1. Explain death to be a state of separation and that the lost are separated from God.

2. Read John 5:24 pointing to the proper points on the chart.

F. Compare and contrast **eternity in the lake of fire, Revelation 20:14-15,** with **heaven, John 14:1-3.**

TRANSITION THOUGHT: Your discussion of heaven.

II. All in group one are headed to the lake of fire.

A. Eternity in the lake of fire is an awful prospect: **Revelation 20:14-15, Psalm 9:17, 2 Thessalonians 1:7-9, John 3:36.**

B. Despite external appearances, God knows who is headed there.

TRANSITION THOUGHT: No escaping the lake of fire for those in group one.

III. No one in group one cannot possibly change his relationship.

A. Most lost people, upon realization of their condition and destiny, attempt to improve their conduct:

43

1. The five major ways: Love, baptism, church, worship and service.

2. *ILLUSTRATE HERE:* Hiring a Christian for $1,000 a day.

3. *ILLUSTRATE HERE:* Pecan tree built from scratch. No life.

B. The confirmation of God's Word.

1. Look at these Scriptures: **Ephesians 2:8-9, Titus 3:5, Isaiah 64:6, Romans 4:5.**

2. *"X"-* out the *good works for salvation* concept.

CONCLUDING THOUGHT: You will explain in next week's lesson how one who cannot help himself can be helped. That lesson is titled *"What God has done for the Lost World."*

3

THREE

What God Has Done for the Lost World

> *"For God so loved the world that he gave his only begotten Son, that whosoever believeth in him should not perish, but have everlasting life.*
>
> John 3:16

TEACHER: HERE ARE YOUR OBJECTIVES FOR THIS LESSON

1. Your first objective is to show your student that based upon the strength of His work on the cross Jesus claims to be God's Savior or Messiah for lost people.

2. Your second objective is to show that Jesus is the only legitimate, qualified Savior.

3. Your third objective is to show that what God did in Christ is all that is necessary to bring lost people into relationship to God.

4. *TEACHER:* Your main and overall objective in this lesson is to present Jesus Christ as the one and only hope for lost sinners.

PRESENTING

LESSON THREE

TEACHER: The title, thought and application accompanying each chapter is for you, not the student. They are here to help you get a better grasp on what you are trying to accomplish and how to go about accomplishing it. Study these. Make them so much a part of you that they become natural to you, just as natural as opening your mouth when your hand heads a spoonful of food toward it.

TITLE

"What God Has Done for the Lost World"

THOUGHT

THROUGH THE GOSPEL JESUS CHRIST HAS DONE EVERYTHING NECESSARY TO BRING LOST MAN INTO A PROPER RELATIONSHIP WITH HIMSELF.

APPLICATION

To cause the student to realize that though he cannot save himself, he can be saved by a savior. To save men from eternal damnation, a savior must meet many careful and specific requirements. Jesus Christ could meet each and every requirement necessary to the savings of saving each lost person without help of any sort from that person. Christ alone is capable of saving sinners.

PRESENTING

Remember to arrive at the house four to five minutes ahead of your appointed teaching time. Exchange warm and friendly greetings, find out how he (she or they) has been since you last saw him, but do not sit down short of the teaching table. Remember that it is important to keep the atmosphere warm and relaxed, but never slouchy and without direction. Do not deviate from your predetermined and announced goal of presenting all the materials in these six lessons within the "one hour per week for six weeks" time frame. To do that you must get started with the teaching on time and never deviate. Do not *idle* or *tread water* too long at any given point. You must get there, get to your task and stay with your mission. Don't be too formal and businesslike about it; be relaxed and at ease, but don't forget or neglect what you are there to do. You are not there merely to socialize or visit in general. You are there to present specific truths within a specific time frame. The student you are teaching needs it, but there are plenty of others out there who need it too. As soon as you can finish with this student, you must go find others to teach. God expects it of you. He has given you a mandate to do it: Mark 16:15, Matthew 28:19-20, etc. Never lose sight of your mission and purpose. You are not out there to do your work; you are there to do God's work. His will is that as many as possible hear these glorious truths.

Once you are seated at the teaching table spread the chart begin with a brief review. Your review should never exceed five minutes; generally three minutes is adequate. Although, each lesson (two through six) should begin with a review sufficient to tie the new lesson into the previous lessons in such a manner as to generate a natural flow of the overall systematic material. Increasingly as you teach, *the big picture* or overview of Christianity should be developing in the mind of your student; not in six disjointed segments, but as one beautiful whole.

My review always starts with a reminder that we are looking at matters as God sees them. As I mention this I point to *God* written at the top of the chart. I always position so my student can read it with me. (If you are sitting across the table from your student, the chart will be upside down to him. As you add new data or point to the chart in a review, flip the chart around so he can see easily what you've entered or are emphasizing.) As I move along in the review I keep pointing to the appropriate points on the chart. I remind my student that the only way we can accurately know what God thinks is through the Bible which is where He has said what He thinks. Thus, we've looked at the Bible and see it to be true through its construction, its prophecies and its claims. God, who must ultimately be faced by every man (point to top left Scriptures), sees the world in two basic groups: those who are not related to Him in any spiritual sense (point to column one) and those who are related to Him as His own saved children (point to column two). I then remind my student that last week we looked at the impossibility of any person in group one getting himself into group two by his own efforts. That is true because human conduct is not the basis God uses in placing a person into either group. Too much evil didn't place those in group one into that awful condition and a great record of good conduct didn't place those in group two into that wonderful condition. Those in group two are there solely and only because they are forgiven and have been made right or *"righteous"* by God Himself. I usually conclude this review by again pointing out the hopeless condition of those in group one. I also re-emphasize how impossible it is for those in that group to change their condition. At this point I am pointing straight at the Scriptures in the lower left hand corner which show the futility of good works or conduct for salvation.

TEACHER: Do not underestimate the value of this review. These are weighty concepts and they need constant clarification and emphasis. They are probably foreign to your student. The review serves as a vehicle to further drive the truth home to him. As I've already pointed out it enables you to link the previously taught lessons to the one you are now teaching however the review is far more than a linking device. Besides linking and further deepening the truth in your student the review also provides an opportunity for you to clarify points in your student's mind or teach a point he totally missed the first time you ran it past him. While you are reviewing, watch carefully. If you see that your student looks puzzled, blank or wants to say something, stop and see what's on his mind. Take a little time and clear it up before you press on.

Also, you do not need to say, *"Now I've concluded our review, I shall proceed to teach you the lesson at hand."* When you've finished the review you'll know it, and your student will know it too, but there is no need to even mention it. Just move right on into the new material in an easy, continuous flow.

Section One

Begin the new material of lesson three by pointing out that one's inability to save his self does not mean he cannot be saved.

A. Explain the word *saved.*

1. *To save* means to rescue or deliver from some danger or peril. A saved person is one who has been rescued or delivered from a danger or peril.

   ILLUSTRATE HERE.

   A drowning child is saved by a lifeguard. A cat trapped on a rooftop is saved by a fireman. A pilot saved himself by parachuting from a crashing plane. In each case, deliverance from a peril occurred.

2. To be *saved* in the Bible sense of the word means to be delivered from damnation in the lake of fire and eternal separation from God. The word is used this way in Ephesians 2:8. Such a deliverance or salvation also means to spend eternity with God experiencing all of the joys and blessings of eternal life in heaven.

B. In the biblical sense of the word one who finds himself in group one cannot *save* himself. Yet it is possible that he can be saved.

ILLUSTRATE HERE.

Tell your student that if he were on a ship from New York to England and the ship sank in the mid-Atlantic Ocean, he'd face a very real danger and peril of dying. It would be utterly impossible to swim to shore. Even if he were blessed to have a life boat, he would be unable to survive long enough to make landfall alive. Suspension in the cold water would mean soon death from hypothermia, drowning or maybe even sharks. Even in a life boat survival would not be for long. Lack of food and water plus exposure to the rough seas would soon take even the heartiest life. In terms of saving himself a person in that situation would be in a helpless and hopeless condition.

But that would not mean there could be no help or salvation for such a person. Another ship might be in the immediate area and come to the rescue of your helpless and hopeless floating student. In such a case your student would be saved, but not by his own efforts. His salvation would come by the efforts of another.

C. God claims the Jesus of the Bible is the Savior who alone can get hopelessly lost men and women out of group one and into the saved condition of group two. They cannot save themselves but He can save them.

   1. *TEACHER:* As you are making this point you should begin adding the **cross** to the chart as illustrated at the end of this chapter.

   2. Right here I get really intense and personal with my student. I tell him that Jesus is not the only one who has claimed to be a Savior. Through the ages of history there have been many who claimed to be saviors. I tell my student that it would be the tragedy of tragedies for any man to put his confidence in a savior only to find out too late at the judgment of God that the one upon whom he depended for salvation was a fraud and no savior at all. That would mean no salvation for all who depended upon that savior and no salvation means eternity in the lake of fire. I thus say to my student, *"Suppose Jesus is not the Savior? Suppose He is a fraud, an impostor? Where does that place all Christians?"* I tell my student that if I'm going to sit here and teach him that Jesus is the Savior and ask him (my student) to base his whole hope for deliverance upon Jesus as his Savior, then I owe it to him to show that Jesus really is the only legitimate, qualified Savior. Therefore, I am going to spend time showing him that what God did in Christ proves Him to be the one, and only one, who can save men. He alone can move a person in group one into group two.

Section Two

At this point tell your student that the evidence establishes Jesus to be God's only Savior.

A. The work that Jesus did whereby He can save sinners is called the *gospel.*

1. Write **Gospel** on the chart as shown and have your student turn to **Romans 1:16** which you also add to the chart. This is a critical passage. I always have my student turn there and look at it as I quote or read it.

   Explain from the verse that the work Christ did is called the *gospel.* Upon the strength of this gospel work God is able to save lost people. Verse 16 calls that work His salvation *"power."*

2. Now turn your student to **1 Corinthians 15:1-4** and add to the chart as shown. This passage is also vital. I always insist that they see it for themselves as I read or quote it.

   First explain from verses 1 and 2 that the *gospel* is the means whereby we are *"saved."* Do not let the phrase *"If ye keep in memory what I preached unto you, unless ye have believed in vain"* confuse you or your student. With that phrase Paul was simply saying that if they had not believed the gospel he preached (which he defined in the next two verses), then their belief was vain. In other words it is not enough just to believe in anything called *the gospel.* Salvation comes only from believing *"the gospel"* as defined here.

   From verses 3 and 4 show your student the Bible definition of *"the gospel of Christ."* It is the fact that Christ (1) **died**, (2) **was buried** and (3) **rose again**. As you point out these three segments of the gospel add them to the chart as illustrated. Make sure your student realizes the saving gospel of Christ is not merely the whole Bible or some good emotional illustration. It is the fact of the death, burial and resurrection of Jesus Christ. God saves sinners (moves people from column one to column two) wholly or solely upon the strength of that work of Christ. The sinner's conduct, for the better or the worse, has absolutely nothing to do with his relationship to God.

B. As to whether or not Jesus really is the Savior of God, thus making this *gospel* work effective to the saving of the lost, 1 Corinthians 15:3 and 4 brings up a means of verification. This passage says there is a way by which we can check the evidence which supports Jesus' claim to be the promised Messiah. The key phrase is that Jesus did what He did *"according to the scriptures."*

1. Explain to your student that there are many other proofs that Jesus is the Messiah. John 5:31-39 specifically mentions five. They are:

   a. Jesus' own claim to being the promised Messiah.

   b. The testimony of John the Baptist.

   c. The miraculous works Jesus performed.

   d. The direct confirmation of the Father.

   e. The testimony of the Old Testament Scriptures. It is this latter line of proof to which Paul referred in 1 Corinthians 15:3 and 4.

2. What both Jesus and Paul are pointing out is the fact that the Old Testament gives us a set of qualifications for the Messiah or Savior of God. God does not ask us to believe that the Jesus of the Bible is the Savior just because He said He was or because Paul said He was. They say compare Jesus point by point with all that the Old Testament predicted the Messiah would have to be. If you find Jesus qualifying at every point (not just most points), then you know He is the Messiah, the real, genuine Savior of God. Only Jesus satisfied every detail at every point and is fully qualified. Compare any purported savior or means of salvation with the Old Testament requirements and you'll quickly see that all others are frauds and impostors. Only Jesus of the Bible was exactly what the Old Testament said the Messiah would be. If we could find one place where He failed, we'd know He is not the Savior; but He never failed.

3. At this point start **adding the lines** as shown on the sample chart. The vanishing point of each is the cross.

   ILLUSTRATE HERE.

   Tell your student that the Old Testament is somewhat like a large glove never before known to man. With the Old Testament God set forth a test grid. When those claiming to be saviors come on the scene see if their hand will fit this glove. If the hand doesn't fit, then the supposed savior is a fraud. Such ones can't save themselves let alone anyone else. All others have failed but Jesus didn't fail. Put any other savior to this same test and you'll see instantly how vain and foolish it is to trust him (or it).

C. Tell your student that it would be impossible in a one-hour session like this to look at all the dozens of Old Testament proofs that Jesus is the legitimate, bona-fide Savior or Christ but that you will point out a few.

   1. One fascinating area of consideration was His birthplace. Old Testament Micah said the real Messiah or Savior would be born in Bethlehem of Judah, Micah 5:2. Anyone claiming to be the Savior with a birthplace other than Bethlehem in Judah would not be the real Savior. In Jesus' case just before He was born His mother (Mary) and His foster father (Joseph) were living in Nazareth of Galilee, Luke 2:4. The last thing any *about to be* mother would want to attempt would be a donkey ride or walk through approximately 100 miles of rugged mountainous terrain. However that's what it took for Mary to get from Nazareth to Bethlehem. In spite of the odds against it, at just the right time the Roman Caesar sent out a decree that all his subjects pay a certain tax, Luke 2:1. This Roman Caesar was pagan and didn't even believe in one God let alone the God of the Jews. The Jews with their religion were a constant source of trouble and friction to him and his Roman kingdom. This Caesar was located nearly 1,000 miles from Israel and surely was not trying to decree a decree that would insure the accurate fulfillment of some ancient Jewish prophecy. However his decree necessitated Mary and Joseph taking the long, arduous trip from Nazareth to Bethlehem to pay the tax. They had to go to Bethlehem to pay the tax

because they were both descendants of King David. Ancestry through King David was another requirement for the Messiah, 2 Samuel 7:16. Thus they went to Bethlehem, and surely enough, right on schedule, in exactly the right place Jesus was born, Luke 2:6-7. Later when Herod heard of Jesus' birth and would have killed Him an angel warned Joseph to take Jesus to Egypt, which he did, Matthew 2:16. This enabled Jesus to fulfill Hosea 11:1 which predicted the Messiah would come out of Egypt.

2. Isaiah predicted the true Messiah would have to be virgin born, Isaiah 7:14. Jesus was virgin born, Luke 1:27, 34-35. This requirement alone eliminates all other *would be* messiahs or saviors.

   TEACHER: Be careful that you *do not* bog down here. Do not try to cover all Old Testament prophecies of the Messiah's first advent. Just pick out a few and cover them well. *Do not* try to use one you do not understand well yourself. It is better to handle a simple one well than a complex one awkwardly. Keep emphasizing as you teach this section that Jesus met *every* requirement imposed on the coming Messiah but that no one else has even come close to meeting them. Tell your student the proof is there. All it needs is an examination. You are not asking your student to accept Jesus as the Savior without evidence. No, sir! The evidence is there and it all points to Jesus while it eliminates *every other* contender.

   A few other Old Testament requirements for the Messiah with which you might want to deal, depending on your personal preference, are His lineage through the tribe of Judah, Genesis 49:10, no bones broken, Exodus 12:46, the piercing of His hands and feet, Psalm 22:16, His words on the cross, Psalm 22:1, and His life of sorrow and grief, Isaiah 53:4. There are many, many others.

3. For Jesus to qualify as the true Messiah He had to meet every requirement as the Lamb of God.

   Early in the Bible, Genesis 3, the first man and woman sinned and fell into condemnation by God. Every one of us has followed their example. They sinned, fell into the dire consequences thereof and then tried solve their own problem. They made fig-leaf clothes which didn't hide their nakedness from God. Those fig-leaf clothes are symbolic of human efforts, good works and better conduct. God came on the scene, killed an animal (probably a lamb) and made clothes for Adam and Eve. The death of the innocent animal in the place of Adam and Eve foreshadowed the coming substitutionary work of the Messiah. Back in Genesis 3:21 God was symbolically saying the Messiah would have to die as the innocent for the guilty in order for sinners to be saved. Add **Genesis 3:21** to the chart as shown.

This point is again symbolically established in **Genesis 22:1-14**. Add this reference to the chart. God commanded Abraham to offer Isaac on Mount Moriah. As Abraham took Isaac the lad saw the sacrifice wood and the fire to burn it, but he saw no sacrificial lamb. He thus asked in verse 7, *"Where is the lamb for a burnt offering?"* Abraham answered, *"My son, God will provide himself a lamb for a burnt offering,"* verse 8. God did provide a ram caught by his horns in a thicket, verse 13. Abraham offered that innocent sheep in guilty Isaac's place. The typical teaching is again the substitutionary sacrifice of the innocent for the guilty. This is teaching by type and foreshadow concerning the coming Messiah. After offering the ram Abraham said, *"In the mount of the Lord it shall be seen,"* verse 14. Notice the *future* tense. It was later at that place that the Messiah (who was God Himself) would die on the cross for sinners even as the ram had died in the place of Isaac.

This Lambship typology is further established in **Exodus 12**. Add the reference to the chart. The angel bringing death was about to pass through the land of Egypt. Only those with the blood of an innocent lamb without blemish applied to the doorposts of their houses would escape mortal death. The perfect, spotless lamb is a pre-figure that Messiah would have to be sinless. The shed blood of the lamb said Messiah would have to give His blood. The blood on the doorposts said the blood of Christ would have to be personally appropriated by the lost. That occurs at the point of faith.

Case after case of the sacrifice of sheep in the place of guilty worshippers could be cited from the Old Testament. Each example foreshadows the coming Messiah. Perhaps Isaiah 53:7 puts it best, *"He was oppressed, and he was afflicted, yet he opened not his mouth: he is brought as a lamb to the slaughter, and as a sheep before her shearers is dumb, so he openeth not his mouth."* Add **Isaiah 53:7** to the chart as shown.

D. Help your student see that each of these requirements and symbolic foreshadows is designed to point men to Jesus Christ and to convince them that He and He alone is the Savior of lost people.

1. Turn your student to **Hebrews 10:1** and add to the chart. From this verse show him that the Levitical offering of sheep or other sacrifices for sinning Jews never took away even one sin. These sacrifices were not designed to take away sin. They were designed to point sinners forward to the coming Messiah.

ILLUSTRATE HERE.

Show your student a picture of your mate or a friend. You can point to a picture in his house. Explain to him that the picture is not the person, not the real thing, just a likeness to point to the person. Nobody hugs or shakes hands with a picture.

Likewise, the law with all its sacrifices was not a means of salvation. No system of good works then or now is a means of salvation. Salvation is in a person, a Savior and His name is Jesus. All those sacrifices of sheep and goats and bullocks were merely images to point men forward to the real Lamb of God. That Lamb is Jesus. He alone is the real sacrifice for sins. Add **Hebrews 9:12** to the chart and read or quote it.

2. Now, turn your student to **Galatians 3:24-26** and add to the chart. Show him right here in the Bible that all the aspects of the law were to bring men to Christ.

3. Add **John 1:29** to your chart and explain to your student why it made so much sense for John the Baptist to call Jesus *"the lamb of God which taketh away the sin of the world."*

4. Add **Acts 8:32-33** and show your student that the Ethiopian man was reading from Isaiah 53:7. Philip explained to him that the Isaiah references were to *"Jesus,"* verse 35.

Section Three

Affirm to your student that according to God in the Bible, upon the strength of the work Jesus did on the cross, every lost person can be saved.

A. When Jesus went to that cross, He went there as the innocent Son of God to die in the place of all of us who are guilty sinners.

   1. Add **1 Peter 3:18** and read or quote it.

   2. Add **1 Peter 2:24** and read or quote it.

   3. Add **Romans 5:6, 8** and read or quote them.

     TEACHER: You won't need to spend much time elaborating on these verses. In view of the case you've built from the Scriptures these passages speak for themselves.

B. Tell your student that God has already, in Christ, done all the work necessary to save lost people. Nothing needs to be added to it.

   1. Add **Hebrews 10:10-14** to the chart and turn your student to it. Show him from this passage that the Old Testament priests never sat down because they could never cure the sin problem. But Jesus *"sat down"* because His *"one sacrifice"* would *"forever"* be all that would be necessary to conquer the sin problem once and for all.

   2. Finally turn to **John 19:30** and add to the chart. Be sure your student sees this verse. Show him that when Jesus said *"It is finished"* He was not conceding defeat. To the contrary He was expressing triumph and victory. In view of His meeting every Messianic qualification and requirement and in view of the work He was doing on the cross as the fully qualified one He could say, *"It is finished."* Not one work more would ever need to be done to get lost men into a saved relationship with God. That means that when it comes to getting from group one into group two neither baptism, nor church membership, nor good works, nor faithfulness nor any other act of conduct is of any value. No further good from anybody is needed. Jesus has done it all.

AS YOU LEAVE:

1. Tell your student that this concludes lesson three. Explain that next week you will teach a lesson titled *"How to Appropriate What God has done."* Tell him that in that lesson you will explain exactly what God says it takes to make Christ's work personal. Explain too that in that lesson you'll show how any person can know for sure that he is saved and in column two.

2. Encourage your student to review the chart during the coming week.

3. Invite him to church.

4. Rise up and make your way to the door with a warm goodbye and an assurance that you'll be back next week at the usual time.

Lesson Three

Rom. 14:11,12
Rom. 2:2
John 17:17

GOD
1 Sam. 16:7

1. Construction
2. Prophecies
3. Bible Claims
   2 Pet. 1:21
   2 Tim. 3:16
   1 Cor. 2:9,10

GOSPEL
Rom. 1:16
1. Death
2. Burial
3. Resurrection

"NO RELATIONSHIP"

1. Lost
   Luke 19:10

2. Condemned
   John 3:18

3. Unforgiven
   Acts 13:38-39

4. Unrighteous
   Rom. 1:18

5. Dead in trespasses
   and sins
   Eph. 2:1

6. Eternity in the lake
   of fire
   Rev. 20:14-15

Gen. 3:21
Gen. 22:1-4
Ex. 12
Isa. 53:7
Heb. 10:1
Heb. 9:12
Gal. 3:24-26
John 1:29
Acts 8:32-33
1 Pet. 3:18
1 Pet. 2:24
Rom. 5:6-8
Heb. 10:10-14
John 19:30

"RELATIONSHIP"

1. Saved
   Eph. 2:8-9

2. Justified
   Rom. 5:1

3. Forgiven
   Eph. 1:7

4. Righteous
   Rom. 3:22

5. Eternal Life
   John 5:24

6. Heaven
   John 14:1-3

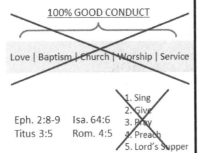

100% GOOD CONDUCT

Love | Baptism | Church | Worship | Service

Eph. 2:8-9   Isa. 64:6
Titus 3:5   Rom. 4:5

1. Sing
2. Give
3. Pray
4. Preach
5. Lord's Supper

STUDY SHEET & LESSON PLAN
LESSON THREE

TITLE

"What God Has Done for the Lost World"

THOUGHT

THROUGH THE GOSPEL JESUS CHRIST HAS DONE
EVERYTHING NECESSARY TO BRING LOST MAN INTO A
PROPER RELATIONSHIP WITH HIMSELF.

APPLICATION

To cause the student to realize that though he cannot save himself,
he can be saved by a savior. To save men from eternal damnation, a
savior must meet many careful and specific requirements. Jesus
Christ could meet each and every requirement necessary to the
savings of saving each lost person without help of any sort from that
person. Christ alone is capable of saving sinners.

BIBLE VERSES TO MEMORIZE

Romans 1:16 *"For I am not ashamed of the gospel of Christ: for it is the
Power of God unto salvation to every one that believeth; to the Jew first, and also
to the Greek."*

1 Corinthians 15:3-4 *"For I delivered unto you first of all that which I also
received, how that Christ died for our sins according to the scriptures; And that he
was buried, and that he rose again the third day according to the scriptures."*

Isaiah 53:7 *"He was oppressed, and he was afflicted; yet he opened not his mouth: he is brought as a lamb to the slaughter, and as a sheep before her shearers is dumb, so he openeth not his mouth."*

John 1:29 *"The next day John seeth Jesus coming unto him, and saith, Behold the Lamb of God, which taketh away the sin of the world."*

Hebrews 10:12 *"But this man, after he had suffered one sacrifice for sins for ever, sat down on the right hand of God."*

John 19:30 *"When Jesus therefore had received the vinegar, he said, It is finished: and he bowed his head, and gave up the ghost."*

OUTLINE

LESSON THREE

I. **Even though one cannot save himself, he can be saved.**

    A. Explain *saved.*

        1. *To save* = To rescue or deliver from a peril.

            ILLUSTRATE HERE: Drowning child saved by a life guard.

        2. The Bible sense of *saved.*

    B. One cannot *save* himself in the Bible sense of the word.

       ILLUSTRATE HERE: Ship sinking in the mid-Atlantic Ocean.

    C. God says the Jesus of the Bible can save lost men.

       TRANSITION THOUGHT: Time showing student that what God did in Christ will change men from group one to group two.

II. **The evidence establishes Jesus to be God's only Savior.**

    A. The *gospel.*

        1. God saves sinners upon the strength of the gospel. **Romans 1:16**

        2. The gospel is (a) the **death,** (b) **burial** and (c) **resurrection** of Christ. **1 Corinthians 15:1-4**

B. *"According to the scriptures"* provides a means of verification. **1 Corinthians 15:3-4**

    1. Five specific proofs. **John 5:31-39**

    2. The Messiah must qualify at every point.

    3. **Add vanishing point lines.**

    ILLUSTRATE HERE: The hand that fits the glove.

C. A look at only a few of the requirements Messiah must meet.

    1. His birthplace. **Micah 5:2, Luke 2:4, Luke 2:1, 2 Samuel 7:16, Luke 2:6-7, Matthew 2:16, Hosea 11:1.**

    2. Virgin born. **Isaiah 7:14** with **Luke 1:27, 34-35.**

    3. The Lambship typology. **Genesis 3:21, Genesis 22:1-14, Exodus 12, Isaiah 53:7.**

D. All requirements and symbolic foreshadows designed to point men to Christ and convince them that He alone is the Savior. **Hebrews 9:12.**

    1. A foreshadow of the real. **Hebrews 10:1.**

    ILLUSTRATE HERE: A picture of someone is not the real someone.

    2. The law designed to bring men to Christ. **Galatians 3:24-26.**

    3. The significance of John the Baptist's statement in **John 1:29.**

    4. *TRANSITION THOUGHT:* Philip's explanation of **Isaiah 53:7** in **Acts 8:32-35** to the Ethiopian man.

III. **God says He can save anyone upon the strength of Christ's work on the cross.**

A. Christ, the innocent, went in place of man, the guilty. **1 Peter 3:18, 1 Peter 2:24, Romans 5:6, 8**

B. Christ did all the work. Nothing needs added to it.

    1. Christ finished the work *"forever"* by *"one sacrifice."*
        Hebrews 10:10-14

    2. *"It is finished."* **John 19:30**

CONCLUDING THOUGHT: Next week's lesson is titled *"How to Appropriate What God has done."* It will show how to make this great work of Jesus Christ personal.

4

FOUR

How to Appropriate What God Has Done

"He that believeth on the Son hath everlasting life: and he that believeth not the Son shall not see life; but the wrath of God abideth on him.

John 3:36

TEACHER: HERE ARE YOUR OBJECTIVES FOR THIS LESSON

1. To first show your student that the only way to get into a "relationship" with God is to believe on Jesus Christ as personal Savior.

2. To then show your student that the New Birth occurs at the point of belief or faith in Jesus Christ.

3. Your third objective is to help your student to determine for sure whether or not he has believed.

65

4. Your main objective is to lead your student to believe on the Lord Jesus Christ as his own personal Savior, if he has not previously done so.

   TEACHER: This is the most important lesson of all and this is your most important objective of the six lessons. Pray for wisdom from God in handling the truth well at this point.

5. Another objective of this lesson is to show your student the basis of certainty or assurance in his salvation.

6. A final objective of this lesson is to leave your student with the realization and assurance that his relationship with God is permanent.

PRESENTING
LESSON FOUR

TITLE

"How to Appropriate What God Has Done"

THOUGHT

FOR THE GOSPEL WORK OF CHRIST TO BE OF
PERSONAL VALUE TO ANY INDIVIDUAL IT MUST BE
RECEIVED BY FAITH.

APPLICATION

To make sure the student understands what belief in the sense of
trust is and to bring him face to face with whether or not he has
believed. This is primarily accomplished through a careful
examination of John 3:36. During this examination all lost students
should be greatly encouraged to believe.

PRESENTING

After you arrive and exchange the customary greetings begin your
review. A brief rehearsing of previously taught information similar to
that offered at the start of lesson three is in order. Your review
should end with emphasis on the fact that everything necessary for
the salvation of lost people has already been done by Jesus Christ.
The only reason any person remains lost is because he has not
appropriated personally the work of Christ as his very own.

TEACHER: I cannot overemphasize to you that this lesson is the
pivotal lesson of the series. All of the first three lessons are just

groundwork to get you here. If your student is lost, this will probably be the best, most likely opportunity you or anyone else will ever have to win him to Christ. If you've done your previous work well and you present the truths of lesson four well, the impact of God's truths is behind you. They are the truths of the Holy Spirit of God and they are convicting and weighty indeed. Do your best to be a yielded tool of God in presenting these truths. If your student is lost and you do not reach him here, the truths of lessons five and six will all be only academic to him. (Yes, you'll need to go ahead and teach them. They provide additional opportunities to bring your student to the point of faith. However until he comes to Christ, he is doomed regardless of what else he knows or does. This lesson is crucial.)

Section One

Flow right from your review into the fact that the one thing God asks of lost sinners is to believe on Jesus Christ as personal Savior.

A. I remind my student (as I write **BELIEVE** in the appropriate place on the chart) that the world and even various religious groups which call themselves "Christians" insist on a variety of fine acts of conduct to be saved.

    1. Some insist on baptism, others on a faithful output of good deeds.

    2. Many say membership in their church is essential to salvation. Others say you haven't received salvation, if you have not "spoken in an unknown tongue."

    3. Most people and religious groups would say you simply won't make heaven if you don't live a good enough life.

B. But, I tell my student that I want to show him right out of the Bible what God says it takes to make the work of Jesus Christ his very own and to thus be saved. At this point I march through several verses letting the Word of God speak for itself. As I do I write the verses on the chart as illustrated.

    1. Add **Acts 16:30-31** to the chart and point out (1) the direct question on how to be saved and (2) the exact answer which are both given in this verse.

2. Add **John 5:24** to the chart. It is effective to point to the appropriate points of comparison and contrast on the chart as you quote or read this verse.

3. Add **John 3:15-18** to the chart. As you read or quote these verses (with your student looking at the passage), emphasize *"believe"* each time it occurs (five times) in this short passage. Really drive home to your student that nothing else is required and nothing short of belief will work; just *belief.* That's all! Emphasize that this is very different from what most of the world thinks but this is what God has said in writing.

Section Two

Next, tell your student that at the point of belief or faith, the New Birth occurs. (Write **NEW BIRTH** on the chart as shown.)

A. Show him from the Scriptures that this is true.

1. Write **John 3:1-14** on the chart and ask your student to turn there. Show him that Jesus is talking. He said in verse 3 that a man *"cannot see the kingdom of God"* and in verse 5 that a man *"cannot enter into"* it apart from the New Birth. Show him that Jesus said in verse 7, *"ye must be born again."* Explain from the text that Nicodemus didn't understand what being born again meant. The text clearly shows he was thinking in physical terms only. However Jesus explained that a spiritual birth is just as essential to spiritual, eternal life as a natural birth is to physical, mortal life. Point out Jesus' explanation to Nicodemus that looking to Jesus, who would be lifted up on the cross in faith, results in spiritual healing or deliverance, verses 14-15. Jesus called that deliverance the *"new birth."* The children of Israel looked in faith to Moses' brass serpent for physical deliverance from death by snakebite; those facing the second death of eternity in the lake of fire look to Jesus' work on the cross for spiritual salvation or deliverance. Believing on Jesus Christ is equivalent to the New Birth because the new birth occurs in the heart at the instant one believes. This is Jesus' explanation of the *"new birth"* to Nicodemus and to all men.

2. Next turn your student to **1 John 5:1** and write it on the chart. Show your student that this verse plainly says, *"He that believeth that Jesus is the Christ is born of God."* There can be no doubt that the New Birth occurs at the point of faith.

B. Explain to your student that God is using family imagery in the Bible to illustrate a spiritual truth.

1. The use of imagery, parallelism or analogies is a very common teaching device. Jesus used it often as in the parables. A physical object was used to teach and illustrate a spiritual truth. Jesus likened the Word of God to seed, believers to sheep and hard hearts to stony ground.

2. One of the more extensive parallels of the Bible is the parallel between the physical family and the spiritual family. It is seen not only in the words of Jesus but also in the words of Paul, Peter and others. *"Born," "father," "children," "brethren," "sons"* and *"family"* are all terms we use in discussing physical family relationships. These terms are used also in discussing the spiritual family of God to give us insight into the nature of the spiritual relationship a believer has with God.

   Whereas it takes a natural birth to gain entrance into and establish relationship in a physical family, likewise Jesus taught that it takes a spiritual birth to gain entrance into and establish a spiritual relationship in God's spiritual family. The New Birth makes God *"our Father,"* Matthew 6:9, and establishes us as *"sons of God,"* 1 John 3:2. We are thus *"brethren"* in the Lord, 1 Thessalonians 4:13.

   If the spiritual family of God parallels the physical family (and it does as these Scriptures show), then a parallel examination removes all validity from several erroneously held concepts. At the same time it verifies the concept of salvation by grace. For example, imagine the ridiculousness of the thought that any human could ever work his way into a physical family. Furthermore who would think anyone could ever be good enough to get into a family? The very idea is absurd. Everybody knows there's just one way to get into a natural family and that's by birth. Nobody ever worked his way into a natural family or was good enough to get into one. Only Adam and Eve were not born and they were made by God through special creation. The idea of working and being good enough to get into God's spiritual family is just as absurd and foreign to scriptural teaching as is the works and goodness concept for natural family membership. Yet, the world and many supposed *Christian denominations* tell you to work hard and do good in order to go to heaven.

TEACHER: Make sure you see that your student recognizes how totally foolish and out of line with Bible thinking that is.

While still on the subject of the family parallel, remind your student of how utterly impossible it is for anyone to get out of his natural family. His goodness or badness has nothing to do with his *relationship* in the family. He's no less a family member if he robs, rapes, murders and is an absolute villain in some penitentiary than if he is living the most wholesome, successful and irreproachable life possible. Yet, when it comes to the spiritual family there are multitudes (many who call themselves Christians) who insist that if you do badly and commit certain sins, you'll be lost again (lose your salvation or family relationship). Point out to your student that such ones are still hung up on the "good conduct for salvation" concept. Such ones have not yet given up on "self" with its "conduct" and placed themselves at the mercy of God for His help. The fact is that conduct has nothing to do with family relationship, spiritual or physical. Birth alone establishes family relationship and birth establishes relationship forever, physically and spiritually. There is no greater chance that one can get out of a bloodline spiritual family relationship (the kind we have with God through the blood of Christ) than there is that one can get out of a bloodline physical family relationship. In both cases, the possibility is zero.

TEACHER: Establish these family points well. All along you've been systematically teaching the security of the believer. It is integrated into all of these lessons, especially the first four, but here the case is growing stronger. At this point you have a real opportunity to drive home the point in a very powerful yet easy-to-grasp way.

Section Three

Now tell your student that you are going to present a specific way to determine for sure whether or not a person is saved.

A. Explain that you are going to focus in on John 3:36 to illustrate this point.

   1. Ask him to turn there.

   2. You should flip the chart to the backside at this time. Write **John 3:36** and **HE THAT BELIEVETH ON THE SON HATH EVERLASTING LIFE** as illustrated.

   3. Explain that you are going to diagram John 3:36 in a way similar to what is done in an English grammar class. Tell him that John 3:36 is only one of many similar Scriptures which establish the same point. This verse was chosen because it is so clear and easy to illustrate.

B. Here is how to teach and illustrate John 3:36 and help a person determine exactly where he stands in relationship (or lack thereof) to God.

   1. First add **1 John 5:13** to the chart. Turn there and show your student from this verse that we can *"know"* for sure that we are saved. Add **know**. There is no reason why anyone should remain uncertain about this matter. Some say that it is not possible for anyone to know for sure that he is saved. God says you can *"know."*

   Also, from 1 John 5:13 show that we can know because of that which is *"written."* In other words God has given us a measuring device and that device is clear-cut Scripture which says exactly what it takes to be saved. If we had no written word on the subject, we could never be sure whether or not we are saved, but we do have the written Word and we can be sure.

72

ILLUSTRATE HERE.

I hold up my pen and ask how long my student thinks it is in inches. I point out that if I should ask ten different people, I'd probably get ten different answers. But there is a way to get us all together on the length, to take out the guess work. We can measure the pen with a ruler and tell exactly how long it is. Likewise, we can measure ourselves spiritually by God's ruler which is that portion of His written Word which addresses the subject. In so doing, we take out all the guesswork. We can know conclusively that we are saved. However the measurement may reveal conclusively that one is lost.

2. Next point your student to the statement John made in John 3:36 and which you have written on the flipside of the chart. Explain that John 3:36 gives both the positive and the negative sides of the same issue. The positive statement is that you have everlasting life, if you are a believer. The negative statement says you do not have everlasting life, if you are not a believer. For illustration purposes you are going to approach the issue from the positive side.

   At this point, **draw the vertical line**, as shown, between *"Son"* and *"hath."* Tell your student that this is really an *if/then* proposition from God. He is saying here that if you believe on the Son, then you have everlasting life. Note well, this is what God says about it. This is not the opinion of a man or group of men.

3. Next **draw the inverted horizontal parenthesis** under *"hath everlasting life"* and write **God's Part** as illustrated. Explain to your student that only God can give eternal life. It cannot be bought or manufactured. It is an observable scientific fact that life comes from life. The only place to get eternal life is from the eternal God. He has said right here in John 3:36 that every person who believes on Jesus Christ *"hath"* everlasting life.

   Discuss *"hath"* with your student. That's old English for "has." That means right now, present tense. Believers are not just going to be saved and get everlasting life when they get to heaven. They have it right now. The body is still mortal, but the spirit has everlasting life. This further verifies the fact that a person can know he is saved right now. He does not have to wait until he physically dies to learn where his spirit will go: to heaven or to the lake of fire.

Next, discuss *"everlasting life."* Remember that one of your objectives for this lesson is to leave your student with the realization and assurance that salvation or relationship with God is permanent. That concept is inherent in the whole plan of eternal redemption which you've been teaching, but here is a place where the focus is directly on that point. So go heavy on the eternal security of the believer right here. Deal with the word *"everlasting."* Remind your student that God says what He means and does not choose the wrong terminology to express His truths. He didn't use *"everlasting"* when He should have used *temporary*.

ILLUSTRATE HERE.

In a somewhat comical fashion, I sometimes tell my student that beauticians misuse terminology in describing their work. Ladies go to their beauticians to get a *permanent* but within a few months they have to go back and get another *permanent* because the first *permanent* wore off. Anyone who thinks much about that would realize that those *permanents* would better be called *temporaries*. They are really not "permanent" at all. God does not deal in such misuse of terms. He calls the life He gives every believer *"everlasting"* and that's exactly what it is. It is not temporary. All who get it have it forever. Otherwise, it would have been only temporary.

TEACHER: At this point add **Romans 8:31-39** to the chart as shown and quote or read it. It is loaded with affirmations that believers are eternally secure in Christ. I sometimes use John 6:35, 37, 39 and 40 to further validate this point. I particularly point out Jesus' words in Verse 39, *"I should lose nothing."* I ask my student, "How many would he have to lose to make this a lie?" I then answer my own question by saying, "Just one." Then, I say, "If there ever has been, is or ever will be one person who was saved but who lost his salvation and thus became "unsaved" again, then Jesus lied in John 6:39. If He lied there, how do we know He did not lie in many other places?" The truth is, He did not lie in John 6:39 or elsewhere. When He said He would not lose one who came unto Him that's exactly what He meant. That means every person who ever was saved is still saved and always will be saved. Not one is in the slightest danger of losing his *"everlasting life."* Besides, if he did lose it, it wasn't *"everlasting"* but rather *temporary.* In that case, Jesus would be lying again when He used the words *"eternal"* and *"everlasting"* in John 3:16. The fact is God doesn't lie or use the wrong words. When He said, *"He that believeth on the Son hath everlasting life,"* that is exactly what He meant and how it is.

4.   Now that you've dealt with *"hath everlasting life"* you need to drive home a very critical point. It relates to the integrity of God and His Word. A firm grasp of this truth by your student is vital to his personal assurance of salvation.

Remind him that the positive affirmation of John 3:36 is an *if/then* proposition by God. He says if you'll believe on the Son, then you will have everlasting life. Stress the fact that this is "God's" proposition. Now ask your student, "Suppose you, or any person, believed on the Son but did not get everlasting life. Would this proposition be true?" Give him four or five seconds to think on it and then answer it for him by saying, "No. Obviously this claim of God would be false, a lie." Bear down here, teacher. Labor this point. If there is even one person who has believed on the Son but who didn't get or doesn't have *"everlasting life,"* then God lied about it right here in John 3:36. Assure your student that God does not lie. Titus 1:2 says, *"God cannot lie."* This is a true affirmation. Tell your student that what that means to him personally; if he is sure he has believed on the Son, he can be sure he has everlasting life. He is saved and is in group two. Let that soak into his heart. Be sure he sees this point. How can he know he is saved once he has believed on the Son? Because God says he is. Where? Right here in John 3:36. That means assurance of salvation is not based on better conduct, an emotional experience, a feeling that one is saved or deep sincerity. No! People who know

75

they are saved know they are saved because God told them they are. He didn't do so through some mystical voice or via a special note on a rock dropped out of heaven. He told them through the Bible, His provable book. He said so in John 3:36 and in many kindred passages. How do I know I am saved? God says I am! Where? In **John 3:36**. I am in that group that has believed on the Son and He says everyone in that group has *"everlasting life."* I am resting on His promise. If He is lying, then I don't have it. However if He is telling the truth, then I do have it. The evidence says He is telling the truth. I believe He is telling the truth. My salvation is just as good as God's Word. My assurance is based on the integrity of God and His Word, not feelings or my own feeble ability to maintain a great track record of good living. My salvation is just as good as His Word. I've believed on the Son and He says I'm saved. That's equally true of every believer. You can't get it any stronger or surer than that.

TEACHER: Do not try to parrot me in this but do get this part down so well into your heart that you can nail down the flaps right here. You want to be sure your student sees the Word of God to be the basis of assurance of salvation. If you fail to show him that, your failure will likely come back to haunt you further down the road. Before moving on to the next point you want your student to know that if he can be sure he has believed on the Son, then he can be sure he is saved. Once you see he has grasped that truth, move on to the next point.

5. Next, **add an inverted horizontal parenthesis** under *"He that believeth on the Son"* as shown on the chart. Also, add **Your Part** as shown. The first thing you should do after you add *Your Part* is explain that *Your Part* is in no way intended to imply some work or action on the part of anyone in need of salvation. Your explanation will soon show that to be true. *Your Part* is included here because salvation is a personal matter between each individual and God. Two parties are involved: God and you. God does all the saving and you do all the receiving. *Your Part* is simply receiving the great work of God for lost sinners.

After this brief explanation **add the two vertical** lines as shown on the sample chart and enter the **(1)**, **(2)**, and **(3)** as illustrated. Tell your student that *Your Part* is divided into three considerations.

First you will explain *"He."* *"He"* is the subject of this sentence and is a universal pronoun. That means *"He"* includes everybody. The *"He"* of John 3:36 is the same as *"whosoever"* in John 3:16. Add **John 3:16** to the chart at this point. *"He"* or *"whosoever"* includes all the really bad sinners. Nobody is too sinful to be saved. **Isaiah 1:18** is an excellent passage to add to the chart and quote at this point. On the other hand nobody is so good that he does not need to be saved. All of the fine moral, sincere, religious, respectable and upstanding people need to be saved. The *"He"* of John 3:36 includes everybody.

Second I find it best to explain the phrase *"on the Son"* before explaining *belief.* The *"that believeth"* part is more difficult for most people to grasp and is usually where they are *hung up.* I save it until last. At this point you have already given your student almost four hours of teaching much of which has centered on *"the Son."* An explanation of *"on the Son"* should be easy for you and the student. In explaining the phrase *"on the Son"* I flip the chart sheet over to the top page and point to the cross explaining that the phrase *"on the Son"* refers to Jesus Christ. I remind my student that I have already explained the great work of Christ on the behalf of lost sinners. I particularly remind him of the gospel, the work where Jesus shed His blood for sinners, died in their place, was buried and rose again the third day. Having done that, I flip the chart to the back side again and point to *"on the Son."* I tell my student that the faith or believing must be on Jesus Christ. God promises no everlasting life to those who believe in their baptism, their good works, their church, their sincerity or any other such work. The promise of *"everlasting life"* is only to those who believe on the Son. This leads me to explain that it is the "object of our belief," even Jesus Christ Himself, who does the actual saving, not belief itself. A person can believe as strongly as he pleases in the wrong savior and still be lost and headed to the lake of fire. This is in fact the case with all who believe in any other person or in some act or thing than Jesus Christ for salvation. That means all of the people who believe in their baptism, good works, clean living, church affiliation, church involvement or sincerity are lost and headed to the lake of fire. God promised to save all who believe on the Son and no one else. Add **John 14:6** to the chart and quote or read it. Also add **Acts 4:12** and read or quote it.

ILLUSTRATE HERE.

I use this illustration to help establish this point. I point to a table lamp, a toaster or some other electrical item which is plugged into a visible electrical socket. In the case of a table lamp, I point out that the lamp is powerless to shine within itself. The real power which causes the light in the lamp is being generated by an electrical power generator and is flowing from that generator through the plug and into the lamp. I tell my student that if I should plug that lamp into my nose, no light would occur in the lamp. If I should plug it into a dead electrical socket, no light would occur regardless of how much I believed in advance that it would. I emphasize that it is not my belief that makes the light shine; it is the power from the electrical generator that does it. My belief is merely the means by which I hook up to the true source of power. My belief, however strong, is valueless if placed in the wrong power source.

Likewise, belief does not save lost people; Jesus Christ does. He is the one and only true source of spiritual power. Our belief or faith simply plugs us into Him. He then does the saving work in us. For any person to put his confidence or belief in the wrong object is eternally disastrous. One's belief or faith must be in Christ. Otherwise he will never have *"everlasting life,"* but for all those who believe in Jesus Christ, *"everlasting life"* is a reality.

Third explain the *"that believeth"* part of this statement. Your student is likely wondering just exactly what this *"that believeth"* means. He probably thinks he does believe and always has believed. He'd probably tell you in a quick moment that there never has been a day in his life when he didn't believe. He's no infidel or atheist and never has been. So, if he has always believed, then why hasn't he always been saved?

TEACHER: Be careful that you make this point crystal clear. *"Believe"* is used in the Bible (and commonly today) in two major senses. We commonly use *"believe"* to express our acceptance of *facts*. As shown write **Believe** on the chart and add **Fact**. Explain that we believe historical facts and accept as fact things we see with our own eyes. Many also accept the facts related to Jesus Christ. Yes, they believe He was a very real historical character. They believe He really did die on the cross, shed His blood, go to the grave and rose again after three days. They believe He lives today and they believe they are sinners and need to be saved. That's as far as many people have gone and they think this makes them saved, but it does not. There is a second way in which we use the word *"believe"* and that is in the sense of *trust, faith, reliance* or *dependence*. Add **Trust** to the chart as shown. This is the sense in which believe is used in John 3:36. A study of the Greek verb used before translation into English would quickly verify this truth. In John 3.36 God said He will give *"everlasting life"* to all those who trust Him, not to those who merely accept the *facts*. Add **Ephesians 1:3** to the chart and quote or read it. Tell your student that it is one thing to believe a set of facts; it is quite another thing to commit yourself to or trust someone or a thing.

ILLUSTRATE HERE.

If I say to my student, "Do you believe there are jet airplanes at the big Houston airport?" He will no doubt say, "Yes." Anyone who has been there knows planes are constantly coming and going with many on the ground at any given time. In all honesty and sincerity, a student can answer "Yes" to the question. "Although," I say to my student, "if I bought tickets for you to fly on one of those jets, we suddenly enter a new dimension of belief. Once you take the tickets, walk onto the jet, and feel it taxi to the runway and accelerate to such a speed that it leaves the ground and climbs into the sky, you no longer believe merely the fact that this is a jet airplane. You now believe in the sense of trust or faith. You are committed to it. If it goes down, you go down. You are at the mercy of the plane.

This is the sense in which a man must believe in Jesus Christ in order to receive *"everlasting life."* It's not enough to accept the fact that He is the Savior and did what the Bible says He did. Salvation or *"everlasting life"* is in trusting Him, believing on Him in the sense of commitment to Him. Some think because they trust Him every day for help on the job, to provide food, for safety, etc., they are saved. We are not talking here about daily trust in Him for the menial matters of life. We're talking about eternal damnation and eternal life, about being lost or being saved. To receive *"everlasting life"* one must believe or trust Jesus Christ for eternal salvation. We're talking here about trusting Jesus Christ to get your spirit to heaven, not just your body safely to work.

C. Having now explained John 3:36 point by point, tell your student that you will present a little test by which any person can determine for sure whether he is lost or saved.

   1. The first question of this little test is **Am I saved?** Write it on your chart as shown. Explain to your student that if anyone answers that question "No," then he needs to be saved. If a person says, "I'm not sure," he surely needs to become sure. Some things do not matter much but whether or not a person is saved matters. It matters more than any other thing. If a person says, "Yes, I am saved," then there surely must be some reason why he says so. There must be some grounds or basis for such a claim.

   2. Thus, the second question is in order: **How was I saved?** Enter it onto the chart. This question asks what the basis for a claim of salvation is. At this point you have not yet directly confronted your student with the question of where he stands. You will momentarily but here you're presenting this little test as to a third party. So you say, "If a person answers that he is saved because he has been baptized, then we can give him an "X" for failure. That person is not saved. You go down a list of false hopes "Xing" them out in like manner. Include good works, sincerity, church affiliation and involvement, etc. They're the more common culprits. After

80

"Xing" out a list of false answers point out to your student that the only correct answer to this question is "I have believed on the Son." The answer may not be worded in those exact words but the idea must be there. Anyone who has any idea that he was saved in some way other than through believing on Jesus Christ is still lost.

3. At this point write the third question on the chart: **When was I saved?** Explain to your student that you are not necessarily asking for the day of the week or date on the calendar, although it is great if a person knows that information. Many saved people will know. The point of your inquiry with this question is the certainty that there was a time when a person realized his lost condition and did in his heart believe on Jesus Christ as his own personal Savior. Until a person knows there was a time when that happened, he'll never know for sure that it did happen. Thus he'll never be sure of his salvation.

Tell your student that you will now draw a *lifeline* on the chart which focuses attention on the time of salvation. Draw a horizontal line on the sheet and write **Birth date** on the left and **Death date** on the right as shown. Place the arrow point heading right and remind your student that each of us has had a birth date. Furthermore we will all ultimately face a death date. We do not like to face it but we all know it is coming. Place **Now** on the chart as shown. Explain that you are arbitrarily placing the "Now." Most people want it over near "Birth date" but "Now" for him might in reality be nearer his "Death date." Only God knows. We cannot accurately place the "Now." All we know is that "Now" is somewhere between our birth date and our death date and we are heading toward our death date.

TEACHER: Tell your student that you are going to enter today's date and time on the chart. That will be whatever the date and time is when you are teaching this lesson. Tell your student that you want him to look back over his life from birth till now and that you want him to locate the time that he was saved: truly believed on the Son in the sense of trust. Tell him that while he is thinking on it you want to share this real life illustration.

ILLUSTRATE HERE.

In a certain church in about 1968 a young lady about fifteen years old came forward at the invitation. She had been a member of that church for several years. She had grown up in a Christian home and was unusually knowledgeable of the Scriptures. She was a fine asset to the youth department with her good attitude and continuous flow of good works. But the young lady was troubled about her spiritual condition. She had doubts about her salvation. The problem seemed too complex to handle in a brief invitation conversation. The pastor asked her to meet with him that afternoon. After a thorough discussion of how to be saved the pastor went through these three questions. At first the answers of the young lady were good. When he asked about her salvation she told him she had been saved during a morning service at a certain Baptist church in another city. She was about eight years old at that time. The pastor asked her if she had ever truly *"believed on the Son"* before that experience at eight years old. She said, "No." He then asked her if she had ever *"believed on the Son"* since that experience. She replied that she had not. She had not thought there was a need to do so since she had been saved at eight years old. The pastor pointed out to her that she had just told him that from birth till now she had never *"believed on the Son"* unless it happened that Sunday when she was eight years old. He pointed out to her that if it didn't happen then she was lost. She could see that he was right.

He then focused on that Sunday when she was eight. He asked her if she really put her faith in Christ during the singing and or during sermon. She said she didn't. During that time she was really convicted and knew she needed to be saved but she said she thought she'd be saved at the invitation. The pastor then asked her if she had believed on the Son when the invitation started or as she walked forward. She seemed a little stunned at the question. She said "No." She thought people got saved *down front.* He then asked her what happened when she arrived *down front.* She explained that she met the preacher and tried to agree to whatever he asked her. She said she was so scared *in front of all those people* that she didn't really know just what he asked her. She simply agreed to whatever he said and hurried on over to put her name and address on a membership card. The pastor asked her if at any point during that encounter with the preacher, she in her heart came face to face with her lost condition and really believed on Jesus Christ as her personal Savior. She said in all honesty she knew she didn't. She was too afraid. Her focus was not on her lost condition and Christ who alone could save her. She was thinking only of that preacher and all those people. She was emotional and hurrying to get it over and done. The pastor then asked her if she believed on the Son while she sat there filling out the card. She said "No." She explained that going through that experience there at the front with the preacher had gotten her saved.

The pastor then said to the young lady, "You told me you never believed on the Son before that Sunday back there when you were eight years old and you told me you never believed on the Son since. Now you've just told me you didn't believe on the Son that Sunday when you were eight. What you have just systematically told me is that in all of your life from your birth date until now, you've never *'believed on the Son.'* Yes, you went up front, were baptized and have been a fine young lady active in church, but you have never done the one thing God asks lost people to do. You have never *'believed on the Son'* and He cannot and will not save you until you do." No wonder she had no assurance; she wasn't sure she had believed on the Son. Until you are sure you have *"believed on the Son"* you can never be sure you are saved.

This young lady is typical of lots of people. When they do a careful inspection of their supposed point of salvation they find they did a whole lot of religious things but left out the one thing God requires. They went forward at the invitation, felt really sorry for their sins, wept, prayed and went through a very emotional experience; but they never *"believed on the Son."* All that other *stuff* is superfluous if a person does not *"believe on the Son."* It all amounts to zero and gives no one salvation or assurance. Only believing on the Son can give anyone salvation and the assurance thereof with Bible backing.

In the case of the young lady the pastor asked her to, right there in that office, forget him. He explained to her that the matter of her salvation was not a matter between her and the preacher. It was a matter between her and the Lord Jesus Christ. The pastor explained that Jesus was present, eager and willing to save her. He would do so the instant she believed on him as her personal Savior. She closed her eyes where she sat in the corner of that little office. The pastor waited. Tears began to flow down her cheeks and a little time later she said, "I've trusted Him now." The pastor then told her that in view of that decision in her heart she could claim as her very own the promise of *"everlasting life"* as given in John 3:36.

D. **TEACHER:** the time has come for you to get personal with your student about his standing before God.

    1. Ask him point blank where he stands. Flip the chart over to the front side and point to the two possibilities as you ask the question.

    2. If he says he is saved, ask him to tell you about it, when and where and how it happened. Don't be offensive and make it appear that you do not believe him. Don't put yourself in the role of a cross-examination attorney. By this time you should have a good rapport with your student and you should present your question as a friend who is interested in sharing the greatest experience of his life.

    3. If he says he is not saved, ask him to believe on the Son right there on the spot. Stop. Do what the pastor did with the young lady. Tell them to forget you and that Jesus Christ is standing there this moment able and wanting to save him. Tell him you are going to simply wait a moment while he and the Lord take care of this all-important business.

    4. If your student seems uncertain about whether or not he really trusted the Lord at some previous point, warn him about what a dangerous matter it is to be uncertain. Tell him that above all things he needs to settle the matter once and for all. I advise people, who look back carefully at a previous experience and are still not certain about what they really did, to trust the Lord now. I explain to them that if they trust the Lord now, it won't undo what might have happened back then. The Lord knows what really happened back then. If trust occurred then, trust now won't at all hurt or undo what happened then. But if trust didn't happen then, what happens here and now will make all the difference, not only in this world, but in eternity. It's not God who is uncertain of the individual's salvation; it is the individual. An individual may never be certain of what happened back there, but he can be certain of what happens here and until he is certain he has believed he'll never be certain he is saved.

5. Even with all this some people still seem to be a little uncertain at this point.

TEACHER: One of the things I thus do is to say something like this to them. "Just suppose that before *right now* I had never been saved. I have been saved, in fact, back in October of 1954. But just suppose I'm deceived about what happened back then and have been lost all these years. Well, right here, this minute, I can tell you that I am trusting Jesus Christ as my own personal Savior. With God looking on my heart, He knows I am telling you the truth. I'm telling you here and now that if Jesus Christ in view of His work on my behalf cannot and does not get me to heaven, I won't be there. I have no other hope, no other claim, only Jesus Christ.

Now, just suppose this was the first time I ever reached this decision; according to John 3:36 God would have saved me just now. Of course, it was not the first time I reached that decision. I did that the first time back in October, 1954 and that's when the Lord saved me. What I did here tonight didn't hurt that one bit. I didn't get saved again. I just reaffirmed my faith in Christ, but if was one who was not sure about what happened back then, you can see how important tonight's (today's) decision would be to me." This little exercise really has helped a great many people.

TEACHER: With that backdrop fresh in your student's mind ask him if he can honestly say right here and now his faith, his trust is in Jesus Christ and Him alone. Many will say "Yes." Then, you can point right there on the chart to John 3:36 and ask, "What then does God say you have?" Unless he has been totally out of tune with what you've been doing this hour he can't help saying, *"Everlasting life."* If this is the first time this student can be sure he made this decision I emphasize that this is the point to which he can always look back as the time of "When was I saved?" I circle the date on the chart and write down the exact time of day.

6. Close this fourth lesson with one final point. Point out to your student that tomorrow or next week or next year he may doubt his salvation. If he does, what can he do? He can ask himself first, "Am I saved?" He's going to answer that with a "Yes." He can then ask himself the second question, "How was I saved?" He has only one answer for that: "I trusted Jesus Christ as my Savior." Next he can ask himself, "When did I trust Jesus?" To that he can answer with the time and date you've written. Then he can ask himself, "What does God say about me in view of my faith in Christ?" He can answer himself by saying, "God says I have everlasting life." Where does God say that? The answer, "In the Bible right there in John Chapter 3, verse 36." With those unshakeable answers your student can then forget his doubts and go on with his business of serving God. The written Word of God is the finest assurance you can get and all believers have it.

AS YOU LEAVE:

1. Tell your student that this concludes lesson four and that you will be back next week at the appointed time to teach lesson five which deals with fellowship and the right motive for living right. The title of the fifth lesson is *"Rudiments to Fellowship and Fruitfulness with God."*

2. Invite him to church. I do not insist on their coming for baptism at this point. Neither do I discourage it. If he has enough background to know their need, then fine. In many cases your student will be so void of a biblical knowledge of baptism and what it means that to mention it here would be like mentioning

Greek. In the sixth lesson, you are going to teach baptism thoroughly. At that point I will encourage him to come for baptism as one knowing well what he is doing.

3. When a person gets saved I always ask them to bow and let me thank God for saving him. We rejoice together.

4. At this point rise up and make your way to the door.

Lesson Four

Rom. 14:11,12
Rom. 2:2
John 17:17

GOD
1 Sam. 16:7

1. Construction
2. Prophecies
3. Bible Claims
   2 Pet. 1:21
   2 Tim. 3:16
   1 Cor. 2:9,10

GOSPEL
Rom. 1:16
1. Death
2. Burial
3. Resurrection

NEW BIRTH
John 3:1-14
1 John 5:1

"NO RELATIONSHIP"
1. Lost
   Luke 19:10
2. Condemned
   John 3:18
3. Unforgiven
   Acts 13:38-39
4. Unrighteous
   Rom. 1:18
5. Dead in trespasses
   and sins
   Eph. 2:1
6. Eternity in the lake
   of fire
   Rev. 20:14-15

Gen. 3:21
Gen. 22:1-4
Ex. 12
Isa. 53:7
Heb. 10:1
Heb. 9:12
Gal. 3:24-26
John 1:29
Acts 8:32-33
1 Pet. 3:18
1 Pet. 2:24
Rom. 5:6-8
Heb. 10:10-14
John 19:30

BELIEVE
Acts 16:30,31
John 5:24
John 3:15-18

"RELATIONSHIP"
1. Saved
   Eph. 2:8-9
2. Justified
   Rom. 5:1
3. Forgiven
   Eph. 1:7
4. Righteous
   Rom. 3:22
5. Eternal Life
   John 5:24
6. Heaven
   John 14:1-3

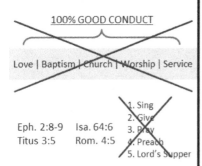

100% GOOD CONDUCT

Love | Baptism | Church | Worship | Service

1. Sing
2. Give
3. Pray
4. Preach
5. Lord's Supper

Eph. 2:8-9   Isa. 64:6
Titus 3:5   Rom. 4:5

STUDY SHEET & LESSON PLAN
LESSON FOUR

TITLE

"How to Appropriate What God Has Done"

THOUGHT

FOR THE GOSPEL WORK OF CHRIST TO BE OF
PERSONAL VALUE TO ANY INDIVIDUAL IT MUST BE
RECEIVED BY FAITH.

APPLICATION

To make sure the student understands what belief in the sense of
trust is and to bring him face to face with whether or not he has
believed. This is primarily accomplished through a careful
examination of John 3:36. During this examination all lost students
should be greatly encouraged to believe.

BIBLE VERSES TO MEMORIZE

Acts 16:30-31 *"And brought them out, and said, Sirs, what must I do to be
saved? And they said, Believe on the Lord Jesus Christ, and thou shalt be saved,
and thy house."*

John 3:15-18 *"That whosoever believeth in him should not perish, but have
eternal life. For God so loved the world, that he gave his only begotten Son, that
whosoever believeth in him should not perish, but have everlasting life. For God
sent not his Son into the world to condemn the world; but that the world through*

him might be saved. He that believeth on him is not condemned: but he that believeth not is condemned already, because he hath not believed in the name of the only begotten Son of God."

1 John 5:1 *"Whosoever believeth that Jesus is the Christ is born of God: and every one that loveth him that begot loveth him also that is begotten of him."*

John 3:36 *"He that believeth on the Son hath everlasting life: and he that believeth not the Son shall not see life; but the wrath of God abideth on him."*

John 14:6 *"Jesus saith unto him, I am the way, the truth, and the life: no man cometh unto the Father, but by me."*

OUTLINE

LESSON FOUR

I.   **God asks only that lost people believe on Him. Add BELIEVE**

   A. God says *"believe"*, others have other ideas.

   B. See it right in the Bible: **Acts 16:30-31; John 5:24; John 3:15-18.**

   TRANSITION THOUGHT: On this issue God's Word is different from what the world thinks.

II. **At the point of belief, the NEW BIRTH occurs.**

   A. The scriptural proof: **John 3:1-14**

   1.   Jesus equated being *"born again,"* **John 3:3, 5, 7**, with believing on Jesus Christ, **John 3:14-16**

   2.   The proof of **1 John 5:1**

   B. God's use of family imagery.

   1.   Parables or parallelism, a biblical common teaching device.

   2.   The extensive family parallelism of the Bible: **Matthew 6:9, 1 John 3:2, 1 Thessalonians 4:13**

   TRANSITION THOUGHT: Bloodline, family relationship.

III. **A specific way to determine whether or not a person is saved.**

   A. **John 3:36.** *"He that believeth on the Son hath everlasting life."*

   B. How to teach and illustrate John 3:36.

      1. **1 John 5:13** proves we can **know** we are saved.

        ILLUSTRATE HERE: Determining the length of a writing pen.

      2. The positive side of John 3:36 is God's *if/then* proposition.

      3. *GOD'S PART:* *"hath everlasting life."*

        "Hath" means now.

        "Everlasting" does not mean *temporary.* **Romans 8:31-39; John 6:35, 37, 39-40**

        ILLUSTRATE HERE: A lady's permanent.

      4. If God is telling the truth, all believers can know they are saved.

      5. *YOUR PART:* *"He that believeth on the Son."*

        "He" is a universal pronoun and includes everybody. **John 3:16** and **Isaiah 1:18**

        "On the Son" relates to the object of belief. Misplaced confidence avails zero. **John 14:6; Acts 4:12**

        ILLUSTRATE HERE: The power that causes an electric light to shine. *"That believeth"* includes fact but also faith. Ephesians 1:13

        ILLUSTRATE HERE: The difference between believing airplanes exist and flying in one.

   C. A simple test with three questions.

      1. **Am I saved?**

      2. **How was I saved?**

3. **When was I saved?**

   The lifeline

   ILLUSTRATE HERE: A young lady in a certain church in 1968.

D. The personal standing of your student.

   1. Ask him where he is.

   2. If he is saved?

   3. If he is lost?

   4. If he is uncertain?

   5. How to help uncertain students.

   6. How to remove doubt.

CONCLUDING THOUGHT: Next week's lesson is titled *"Rudiments to Fellowship and Fruitfulness with God."*

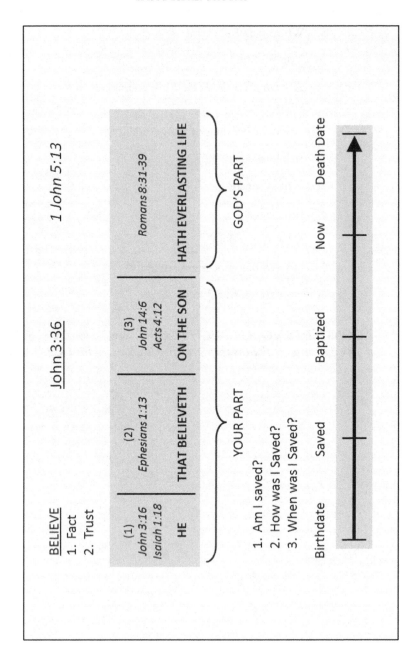

5

FIVE

Rudiments to Fellowship and Fruitfulness with God

"But if we walk in the light, as he is in the light, we have fellowship one with another, and the blood of Jesus Christ his Son cleanseth us from all sin.

1 John 1:7

TEACHER: HERE ARE YOUR OBJECTIVES FOR THIS LESSON

1. Your first objective is to show the difference between *relationship* and *fellowship*.

2. Your second objective is to show that it is not possible to have the quality of life God desires for each of His children apart from fellowship with Him.

3. Another objective of this lesson is to show that conduct will have a direct bearing on a believer's fellowship with God.

95

4. A most important objective of this lesson is to show your student how to stay in fellowship with God.

5. Another objective is to convince your student that love should be his only motive for whatever he does in the work of the Lord.

PRESENTING

LESSON FIVE

TITLE

"Rudiments to Fellowship and Fruitfulness with God"

THOUGHT

ONCE A PERSON IS SAVED HE NEEDS TO LEARN WHAT
IT MEANS TO WALK IN FELLOWSHIP WITH GOD.

APPLICATION

Distinguish between relationship and fellowship and teach your
student how fellowship is lost and regained. Then teach him that
love is the motive for all Christian service.

PRESENTING

Remember to always review. Review will be especially important
here. Last week your student was confronted with his own spiritual
condition before God and he may well have trusted Jesus Christ as
his Savior. He may have questions or uncertainties at this point
which a review will enable you to spot and clear up for him. I would
spend most of this review retouching the points of lesson four. It will
not take you but a minute to remind him that in this study we are
looking at things the way God does. We do that through the Bible.
Briefly point out the big challenge here is how to get from *the group
that is lost* into *the one that is saved*. It is impossible for man to get
himself out of group one and into group two. However God,
through the person and work of Jesus Christ, can change any person

from lost to saved. God works this change with any individual the instant he believes on Jesus Christ. To believe is to trust; and the moment trust in Christ occurs, the lost person is born again spiritually into God's family. There is no other way to be saved but once saved a person can't be lost.

TEACHER: You should tell your student that you are changing directions with this lesson. All through the first four lessons, you have been talking about how to get into God's family, how to be saved. You will now begin discussing what a person does after he is saved. Nothing you'll be dealing with here and in the final lesson has to do with whether or not a person is saved and on his way to heaven. It's one thing to have a baby; it's quite a different thing to rear him to maturity. So in lessons five and six we will discuss what those who are already babes in Christ are to do, how they are to live and act. In these lessons we will not be dealing with what it takes for a person to become a newborn babe in Christ. That's important for your student to see lest he misunderstand that you are now trying to tell him to do something in order to be saved. Make sure he understands that he is already saved and will stay that way regardless of whether or not he ever does another thing good or bad. However God, like any decent parent, is not interested in just getting newborns into his family to live there in infancy with no growth. No. He wants His newborn babies to grow to maturity and fruitfulness in His work. The material you will now present is designed for those already saved, not to get folks saved.

Section One

Tell your student that you will now begin a discussion of _fellowship_ with God. _Fellowship_ is considerably different than _relationship_ to God.

A. Explain _fellowship_ and how it differs from _relationship_.

    1. Write **Fellowship** on the chart as shown and enter **1 John 1.** Explain that fellowship is agreement, accord, harmony.

    2. Contrast _fellowship_ with _relationship_ which speaks of kinship, parentage, lineage and blood connection. Point out that one may have fellowship with people with whom they are not related. Fellowship is speaking of a different aspect of life altogether than relationship.

3. Point out that relationship is established and affected solely by birth. (At this point write **Birth** on the chart and connect to *Relationship* as shown.) On the other hand *fellowship* with God, though initially established by the New Birth, is affected by one's *conduct*. Write **Conduct** on the chart and connect to *Fellowship* as shown. Tell your student that conduct is not unimportant to Christians. Conduct is very important and should always be *good* however good conduct is not to be done in order to be saved. Good conduct should come voluntarily from those who are already saved. Conduct does not affect relationship at all; it does drastically affect fellowship.

ILLUSTRATE HERE.

Use the family analogy. Everybody knows that good or bad conduct has absolutely no bearing upon a family member's relationship to the family. Everybody also knows conduct has a great, great bearing on the fellowship that one has with the family. It seems that almost nobody in physical families has any trouble separating between relationship and fellowship. Yet, in the spiritual realm, big numbers of people are always trying to confuse the two and lump them into one. Confusion right here is why so many think good conduct and works are the way to salvation. They think conduct has to do with relationship. It does not; it relates only to fellowship. One good look at the physical/spiritual family parallel is sufficient to establish this great truth.

B. Explain to your student that God wants His children to always enjoy good fellowship with Him.

1. **1 John 1** is an excellent passage in which God uses the apostle John to call for *"fellowship."* Especially note verse 3.

2. Any parent can easily see how God wants fellowship with His children. God is light. When His children walk in fellowship with Him they are blessed. God doesn't want His children getting away from Him and into ungodly living. He knows they'll get into trouble and spiritual poverty as

evidenced by the prodigal son of Luke 15. God wants His children to enjoy spiritual quality and prosperity in their lives. That is possible only as long as they fellowship with Him in righteousness and truth. Jesus said, *"I am come that ye might have life, and have it more abundantly,"* **John 10:10**. (Add to the chart.) God is not interested in getting you into His family only to have you crash. He wants quality in your life. He thus wants fellowship. He tells us in **Colossians 2:6** to walk with Him. (Add to chart.)

C. Next teach your student that evil conduct has a directly adverse bearing upon a believer's fellowship with God.

  1. **Sin** breaks fellowship with God. Add to the chart. Add also **Isaiah 59:1-2** and turn to the passage. Read or quote it. Explain that sin cannot break your student's relationship with God but it can break his fellowship and cause him plenty of misery. Jeremiah 5:25 is another very clear passage on this subject.

  2. Since sin is a reality of life for all of us, believers included, 1 John 1:8, 10, every believer will find that continuing in unhindered fellowship with God is not as easy as it may at first seem.

  TEACHER: Warn your student not to be too surprised or down on himself when he sins and finds his fellowship with God hampered and not as sweet as it once was. Getting out of fellowship with God is called *backsliding* and it happens because of sin in our lives and sin is a reality of life with which we all contend.

Section Two

Now teach your student that God loves His children. Once one of them gets out of fellowship with Him He takes immediate action to bring that child back into fellowship with Him.

A. He does so by introducing discipline into that child's life.

  1. Write **Discipline** on the chart and enter **Hebrews 12:5-11**.

100

2. Three degrees of discipline are mentioned in this passage: first *"rebuke"*, second *"chasten"* and third *"scourge."* When His Word is read, heard, taught or preached it will rebuke us about sin in our lives. God may bring it to our ears through a variety of means. It may reach us through a preacher, a mate or even an enemy. If we ignore His *"rebuke,"* His discipline will turn more severe. This text mentions *"chastening."* If *"chastening"* does not turn us from our sin, then austere *"scourging"* comes.

3. **TEACHER:** You should now read this entire passage. Ask your student to follow in his Bible. Highlight the fact that *all* of God's children get discipline, *"every,"* verse 6. Also emphasize from verse 8 that anyone who sins against God and receives no discipline is not a son even though he may pretend to be. (Warn your student not to make himself a judge, for God may be administering chastening which he cannot see.) Also highlight from verses 5 and 10 that God's children should not resent and resist the chastening of the Lord for it is always corrective and never punitive. It is always for the child's good and never his hurt. Oh yes, it may hurt but never as much as the consequences of the sin would hurt. God is seeking to correct with His discipline and save His child from evil consequences. From this passage emphasize that the correction and profit come only to those who see what God is doing and turn from the sin, *"them which are exercised thereby,"* verse 11. Those who stiffen their necks and rebel against God get in worse and worse shape until God may have to bring them to an early grave as was the case of some of the Corinthian believers in 1 Corinthians 11:30.

ILLUSTRATE HERE.

I have two sons and a daughter. As they grew up I saw seen evil trends develop in them which I knew would hurt or ruin them in life. What kind of father would I be I had seen such trends and realized the consequences, yet did nothing to correct the problem? Sure, as a natural father, I care about the long-term welfare of my children. How much more does our heavenly Father care about His own spiritual sons and daughters!

B. Now it's time to teach your student what to do once he sins and God's discipline begins. Teach him how to get back in fellowship with God.

1. Tell him there is just one way a believer can get back in fellowship with God. He must confess his sin to God. Write **Confession** on the chart as shown.

2. Now enter **1 John 1:9** and have your student look up the verse.

   TEACHER: If he misses this, he will never be fruitful and happy in his Christian life. He will sin. If he doesn't learn what to do about it, he'll be a spiritual shipwreck. So see that he gets this truth. It is probably the most important truth of all to an effective Christian walk.

   Explain that confession is acknowledging in truth your sin to God. It is not an empty, insincere naming of sin. It is an acknowledgment from the heart that God is right and you are wrong.

   Explain also that confession is to be made directly to God, not the preacher or some other person. Yes, we believe in confession. It is not something only for Catholics. We confess, but not to a man. We confess to God.

   Explain that once we confess in truth, God forgives and *guilt* is gone. Once God forgives there's no need to keep blaming yourself and holding the sin over your own head. According to 1 John 1:7 upon the strength of the blood of Jesus Christ it's gone, forgiven, cancelled.

   TEACHER: Teach your student to confess, not just at church on Sundays or at the end of the day, but moment by moment the instant sin occurs in his life.

3. Now add **Hebrews 4:14-16** to the chart and turn your student to the passage as you read or quote it. Point out to him that Jesus Christ is our High Priest and the one to whom we are to come in confession. Stress that He welcomes our coming. Show him from verse 16 the two things we get when we come to Him in confession. First we get *"mercy."* That's what

forgiveness is, *"mercy."* We sin and He forgives. It's not justice that we get when we come in guilt; it is mercy. Second we get *"grace to help in the time of need."* Not only does our High Priest, Jesus, forgive our sin He also gives us special help for the next temptation and trial. He gives us help deep in the soil of our soul, the place where the sin had its birth and grew. If we had a temper fit, He knows it grew out of a spirit of anger. He thus not only forgives the temper fit but He also gives grace or spiritual medicine to address the spirit of anger from which the fit grew.

Oh yes, Jesus is interested in our well-being and one of His chief ways of helping us is through prayer. So, teach your student to pray. Teach him that in order for him to stay in fellowship with God and be a happy and fruitful Christian, prayer and confession must become an every-day (and often throughout-the-day) part of his life. Confession brings restoration of fellowship. Without it he'll get out and stay out of fellowship.

Section Three

Now tell your student that as a child of God there will be many things God will ask him to do. God wants him to do all that he ever does for one and only one reason. That reason or motive is love.

A. Explain to him that God does not want His children to do good things because they *have to*. He wants them to do right and serve Him because they *want to*. God wants the motive to be right.

    1. Add **Love** to the chart as shown.

    2. Explain that as a child of God we don't *have to* do anything. God wants us to do lots of things. Just as any caring parent wants his child to grow up to be good, honest, respectable and hard-working, God wants those things from His spiritual children. Even when our conduct is awful we're still God's children and going to heaven. Our spiritual birth settled that forever. Will there be discipline? Yes! Will our lives be unfruitful? Yes! Obviously we do not have to serve

God to be saved and go to heaven. Our eternal destiny does not depend upon whether or not we do. However what He has done for us should make us want to serve Him with all our might!

B. Begin adding Scriptures looking at and commenting on them as you go.

1. Add **1 Peter 4:8**. Note that *"charity"* (a Bible word for love) is to be *"above,"* not *equal to* all other character traits in God's children.

2. Add **2 Corinthians 5:14**. This verse shows love to be the motivating (constraining) force of believers.

3. Add **1 Corinthians 13:1-3**. Read or quote these verses carefully as your student follows. They establish beyond doubt that all one does in the service of God is vain, if it be not motivated by love. That means God is not honored by the giving of our money, unless we give it from a heart of love. Giving is not to be done because the church requires it or to impress others. We are not to sing to impress others with our talent or to refrain from stealing or adultery because we might get caught. We are not to go to church because we owe it to the kids or to show off fine clothes or to establish potential business contacts.

4. No! Everything we do is to be done because we love God. Add **1 Corinthians 10:31**. Read or quote it. When one who has been saved thinks back on where he was as a lost sinner and considers the price that was paid in Christ for his salvation, surely love and gratitude should fill his heart. There could never be any higher privilege than giving ourselves out of gratitude in the service of the one who has done so much for us.

5. Serving God out of singleness of heart simply because we love Him is a very practical truth. When we love God and seek to do only what He wants, we do good things. He never wills anyone to do evil. Thus when functioning out of love we find ourselves doing right to please Him, not to please the boss, keep out of trouble with the law or because we *owe*

it to someone. That means we'll do just as good a job when the boss is not around as we would with him looking over our shoulder. That means our neighbor's house is just as safe from us unlocked as it would be locked. We'd never steal a thing even if there were no locks or guards. That means we'd be just as true to our mate if we knew we'd never be found out because we love God and know He wants fidelity in us.

TEACHER: You can name other such considerations as they come to mind. The main thing here is to see that your student sees what a beautiful and practical motive love is. I know the world never will function on love, but if it did, we would never need a great military and defense system. We'd never need locks or police. We'd need no criminal courts, jails and penitentiaries. If love for God was the single motive of the human race, men wouldn't be wronging other men. Love isn't the motive of all men but you can teach your student that it can and ought to be his one and only motive.

AS YOU LEAVE:

1. Tell your student that you are going to conclude lesson five at this point. Point out to him that in the five lessons through now no action has been required. Everything so far has been limited to decisions made in the heart. Though you have taught him how to pray and why he should, you have not asked him to pray, be baptized, join the church or do anything else. Tell him that the next lesson will be a lesson of action. You'll begin explaining some things God wants him to actively do now that he is one of God's children. The title of next week's lesson will be *"Worshipping and Serving God as a Part of One of His Churches."* Tell your student that next week's lesson will begin with a thorough explanation of baptism: what it is and why it should occur.

2. Encourage your student to be in church this Sunday.

3. Then rise up and make your way to the door with assurance that you'll be back at the same time next week to conclude the six lesson series.

Lesson Five

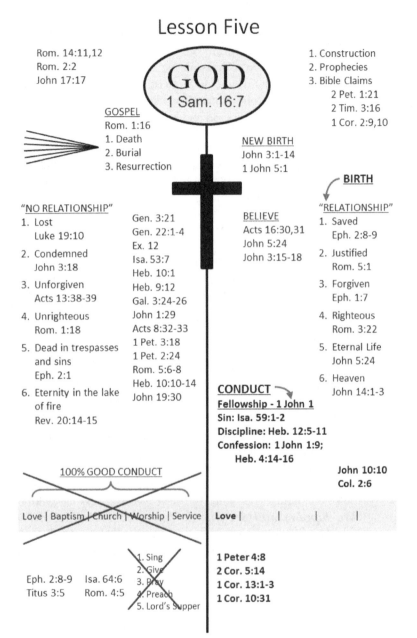

Rom. 14:11,12
Rom. 2:2
John 17:17

1. Construction
2. Prophecies
3. Bible Claims
   2 Pet. 1:21
   2 Tim. 3:16
   1 Cor. 2:9,10

GOSPEL
Rom. 1:16
1. Death
2. Burial
3. Resurrection

GOD
1 Sam. 16:7

NEW BIRTH
John 3:1-14
1 John 5:1

BIRTH

"NO RELATIONSHIP"
1. Lost
   Luke 19:10
2. Condemned
   John 3:18
3. Unforgiven
   Acts 13:38-39
4. Unrighteous
   Rom. 1:18
5. Dead in trespasses
   and sins
   Eph. 2:1
6. Eternity in the lake
   of fire
   Rev. 20:14-15

Gen. 3:21
Gen. 22:1-4
Ex. 12
Isa. 53:7
Heb. 10:1
Heb. 9:12
Gal. 3:24-26
John 1:29
Acts 8:32-33
1 Pet. 3:18
1 Pet. 2:24
Rom. 5:6-8
Heb. 10:10-14
John 19:30

BELIEVE
Acts 16:30,31
John 5:24
John 3:15-18

"RELATIONSHIP"
1. Saved
   Eph. 2:8-9
2. Justified
   Rom. 5:1
3. Forgiven
   Eph. 1:7
4. Righteous
   Rom. 3:22
5. Eternal Life
   John 5:24
6. Heaven
   John 14:1-3

CONDUCT
Fellowship - 1 John 1
Sin: Isa. 59:1-2
Discipline: Heb. 12:5-11
Confession: 1 John 1:9;
Heb. 4:14-16

John 10:10
Col. 2:6

100% GOOD CONDUCT

Love | Baptism | Church | Worship | Service   Love | | | |

Eph. 2:8-9   Isa. 64:6
Titus 3:5   Rom. 4:5

1. Sing
2. Give
3. Pray
4. Preach
5. Lord's Supper

1 Peter 4:8
2 Cor. 5:14
1 Cor. 13:1-3
1 Cor. 10:31

STUDY SHEET & LESSON PLAN

LESSON FIVE

TITLE

"Rudiments to Fellowship and Fruitfulness with God"

THOUGHT

ONCE A PERSON IS SAVED HE NEEDS TO LEARN WHAT
IT MEANS TO WALK IN FELLOWSHIP WITH GOD.

APPLICATION

Distinguish between relationship and fellowship and teach your
student how fellowship is lost and regained. Then teach him that
love is the motive for all Christian service.

BIBLE VERSES TO MEMORIZE

1 John 1:7 *"But if we walk in the light, as he is in the light, we have fellowship
one with another, and the blood of Jesus Christ his Son cleanseth us from all sin."*

Isaiah 59:1-2 *"Behold, the Lord's hand is not shortened, that it cannot save;
neither his ear heavy, that it cannot hear: But your iniquities have separated
between you and your God, and your sins have hid his face from you, that he will
not hear."*

1 John 1:9 *"If we confess our sins, he is faithful and just to forgive us our sins,
and to cleanse us from all unrighteousness."*

Hebrews 4:14-16 *"Seeing then that we have a great high priest, that is passed into the heavens, Jesus the Son of God, let us holdfast our profession. For we have not an high priest which cannot be touched with the feeling of our infirmities; but was in all points tempted like as we are, yet without sin. Let us therefore come boldly unto the throne of grace, that we may obtain mercy, and find grace to help in time of need."*

1 Corinthians 10:31 *"Whether therefore ye eat, or drink, or whatsoever ye do, do all to the glory of God."*

OUTLINE

LESSON FIVE

I. **FELLOWSHIP with God involves a different area than** *Relationship* **to God.**

    A. Explain *"Fellowship."* **1 John 1**

    ILLUSTRATE HERE: an elaboration of the family parallel.

    B. God wants good fellowship with His children: **1 John 1:3, John 10:10, Colossians 2:6.**

    C. Evil conduct adversely affects fellowship with God.

        1. **Sin** breaks fellowship. **Isaiah 59:1-2**

        2. Sin is a reality for all of God's children. **1 John 1:8-10**

        TRANSITION THOUGHT: Sin, a reality with which we must contend.

II. **God takes action to restore broken fellowship.**

    A. He does it with discipline.

        1. **Hebrews 12:5-11.** *"Rebuke," "chasten," "scourge."*

        2. All of God's children receive discipline. It is always corrective.

        ILLUSTRATE HERE: Parents with children.

B. What to do when fellowship is broken.

    1. Confess to God. **1 John 1:9.**

    2. God forgives the sin and gives help to overcome the weakness. **Hebrews 4:14-16.**

    TRANSITION THOUGHT: Confession brings restoration of fellowship.

III. **God wants only one motive to move His children: LOVE.**

    A. Do because you *want to*, not because you *have to.*

    B. Scriptures which teach love as the believer's only motive.

        1. **1 Peter 4:8.** *"Charity"* to be *"above"* all else.

        2. **2 Corinthians 5:14.** Our *constraining* force.

        3. **1 Corinthians 13:1-3.** All efforts worthless unless motivated by love.

        4. **1 Corinthians 10:31.** *Everything* for the glory of God.

        5. A very practical truth.

CONCLUDING THOUGHT: Nothing taught so far has required any action by your student. Next week's lesson is titled *"Worshipping and Serving God as a Part of One of His Churches."* It will discuss actions which God desires of His children. It will begin with a thorough explanation of baptism.

SIX

Worshipping and Serving God as a Part of One of His Churches

> *"Then they that gladly received his word were baptized: and the same day there were added unto them about three thousand souls.*
>
> Acts 2:41

TEACHER: **HERE ARE YOUR OBJECTIVES FOR THIS LESSON**

1. Your first objective in this lesson is to educate your student as to what constitutes a scriptural baptism which is the only baptism God recognizes.

2. Your second objective is to convince your student that he should publicly identify himself with the Lord through baptism.

3. Your next objective is to educate your student that baptism will make him a member of one of the Lord's churches and that he should become an active participant in that church.

111

4. Another objective of this lesson is to educate your student as to what true worship of God is and why he should worship God.

5. Your next objective is to educate your student as to what service to God is and why he should serve God.

6. Your final objective of this lesson is to focus the attention of your student on the natural progression in the order of truth you've presented to him in these six lessons.

PRESENTING

LESSON SIX

TITLE

"Worshipping and Serving God as a Part of One of His Churches"

THOUGHT

A CERTAIN TYPE OF CONDUCT IS NECESSARY TO A CONTINUING FELLOWSHIP WITH GOD AND FOR EFFECTIVENESS IN HIS WORK.

APPLICATION

Cause the student to realize that in order to please God and stay in fellowship with Him proper baptism, church membership, worship and service are necessary. Explain in some detail what these activities are.

PRESENTING

TEACHER: This is your last shot; make it count! I usually spend very little time reviewing to begin this lesson (no more than one minute). There is an automatic review built into this lesson at the end. I save my review until then. I open lesson six something like this. "You will remember that last week I explained fellowship and how our heavenly Father wants us to stay in fellowship with Him. It is only when we are in fellowship with Him that He can bless our lives fully as He desires to do. It is only when we are in fellowship with Him that our lives become really happy and fruitful. I also explained last week that everything we ever do after we are saved, we are to do because love motivates us to do it. Love! It is the main motive which God wants in His children. Tonight (today) I am going to show you the type of conduct God wants in His children." With that brief review I plunge right into my first point of Lesson Six.

Section One

TEACHER: **Your first move in lesson six is to take a good look at baptism.**

A. Tell your student that the first act of conduct God expects of a child of His is baptism.

    1. Add **Baptism** to the chart as shown and put **Acts 2:41** under it. From Acts 2:41 show your student that the first response by these who heard and received the Word of God in this text (the same thing that has happened in this home during these six lessons) was baptism. At this point add **Acts 16:33** to the chart and show your student the case of the jailer in Philippi. The word *"straightway"* means *right away*.

    TEACHER: In a loving and kind but straightforward way instruct your student who has been saved that he should be baptized right away. This is the scriptural order established by God Himself.

    2. Continue by explaining to him that in baptism he will typify the death, burial and resurrection of Christ. Remind him that the death, burial and resurrection of Christ is the *"gospel,"* the work of God whereby he was saved. Add **Romans 6:4-5** to the chart and write **Picture of the Gospel** as shown. Tell your student that when he goes down into the water he will actually act out (pantomime) a burial. Since we bury dead people the burial presupposes a death. Everyone who has seen a funeral knows that is true. By going down into the water of baptism your student will be picturing a death and burial. When he comes up out of the water of baptism he will be picturing or typifying a resurrection. Thus by his baptism he will publicly act out the death, burial and resurrection of Christ. He will become an actor on a stage saying to all the world that he has personally taken advantage

114

of the death, burial and resurrection of Christ. He will publicly declare that his hope is based solely on the gospel work of Jesus Christ. Baptism is the biblical way of becoming a public disciple of Jesus Christ. Baptism doesn't give anyone eternal life; it does publicly declare that he has it. It also testifies of how and where he got it. Until baptism occurs God doesn't consider His child to be a public disciple. Yes, he is a child of God, but a child in secret. More than any other symbol or act baptism marks or identifies people as Christians. It's God's way and you should encourage your new convert to make his new membership in God's family public. Baptism does so. It says the old way is gone and the believer has new life. It also announces the plans of the new believer to walk in newness of life.

B. You should now teach your student what God says it takes to constitute real baptism, a baptism that He would recognize as authentic.

   1. Tell your student that in the opinion of God (and His is the only opinion that really matters) for a baptism to be valid three basic requirements must be met. Point out to him that many "baptisms" are not legitimate. A water event occurs which is called "baptism" but God does not recognize it as valid.

   ILLUSTRATE HERE.

   To be legally valid certain documents have to be notarized. (1) The person who notarizes a document must be certified and thus have legal authority to notarize. If not, documents he notarizes are not valid even though every other detail is correct to the letter. Regardless of his sincerity and good intentions, not everyone can notarize a document. (2) Furthermore legitimacy requires factual integrity. For example, the odometer reading on a vehicle document must be as stated. To claim a vehicle has 50,000 miles when it actually has 75,000 is a crime. It is unlawful to make a dishonest claim. A falsified statement will invalidate a document even though it is notarized. (3) To be valid a notarization must be done in the proper manner. The data must be entered in the right places, there must be witnesses and they must sign the document and do so in the right places. The notary is also required to record the transaction in a special book. Failure by a qualified notary to notarize even factually correct information in the proper manner invalidates the entire transaction.

A valid notarization requires several steps and they must all be done properly. In this example three ways a document can be rendered invalid are illustrated. Failure in any one of the three can render the entire document invalid: improper information, improper method or improper authority. Likewise, as we shall now see, God has established three requirements for valid or legitimate baptism. Failure to meet any one of the three will render the baptism totally invalid.

2. The first requirement for a valid (scriptural) baptism is that the person being baptized must be a believer in Jesus Christ as personal Savior. Write **BELIEVER** on the chart and add **Acts 8:36-37**. Read or quote these verses which clearly show that Philip would not baptize the Ethiopian man unless he was first a believer. The point is that one must be saved <u>before</u> he can be legitimately baptized. That is always the order of truth where baptism is seen in the Bible. That means all the supposed *baptisms* that anyone had before being saved didn't count. They were not valid. That means infant baptism is worthless.

Remember that baptism pictures the death, burial and resurrection of Jesus Christ. It says the person being baptized has personally taken advantage by faith of Christ's death, burial and resurrection. Obviously, a person cannot say that in truth until it occurs. For a person to be baptized before he is saved is a lie by action. He says he's a believer in Christ when in fact he is not. In God's opinion such a baptism is invalid. God views such ones as never having been baptized.

3. The second requirement for a valid baptism is immersion. Write **IMMERSION** on the chart and add **Acts 8:38-39**. Have your student consider the case of the Ethiopian man and Philip again as to methodology. Clearly both went into and came up out of the water. The word *"baptize"* means to

116

cover fully with a liquid. The text proves the liquid to be water. The method of immersion in water is a striking picture of a death, burial and resurrection which is what baptism is designed to picture. Anyone familiar with the gospel of Christ can get the picture when they watch an immersion. However sprinkling, pouring or dampening with a cloth in no way picture the death, burial and resurrection of Christ.

As far as God is concerned those other types do not count. According to what He says in His Bible, people with *baptisms* of that sort have not been legitimately baptized. A person may in fact have been a believer when it happened but the violation of either the scriptural method or scriptural authority invalidated the whole event.

4. The third requirement for a valid baptism is that it be administered by a proper authority. Only a New Testament church has the authority to baptize. Add **AUTHORITY** and **Matthew 28:16, 19-20** to the chart as shown. The authority to baptize was not given to individuals; it was given to Jesus' church collectively. 1 Corinthians 12:28 says the first members of Jesus' church were the apostles and Matthew 28:16 will show these to be the ones to whom the authority to baptize was given. See it in Matthew 28:19-20.

Jesus initiated His church during His earthly ministry (Matthew 16:18). That was almost 2,000 years ago. History proves that from the church Jesus established in Jerusalem to the present there have been churches in continuous operation just like that first church. There never has been a time from Matthew 16:18 until now when there have not been churches on earth in one location or another just like the one Jesus built in Jerusalem. These have authority to baptize; no others do.

The one type of church which can trace its lineage in like kind all the way back to that church in Jerusalem is a Baptist church. All the others are breakaways: the Catholics at least 250 years later, the Lutherans over 1,500 years later and the Presbyterians, Methodists, Church of Christ, Pentecostals, non-denominationalists and a host of others less than 300 years ago. It's obvious on the surface that a church which started with a man as its founder (Martin Luther, John Calvin, John Wesley, Alexander Campbell, etc.) 250 years, 1,500 years or 1,800 years after Jesus Christ cannot possibly be legitimate. Jesus founded a particular kind of church and gave exclusive authority to it and its descendants to baptize believers by immersion. Not one of those late-comer churches has authority to baptize anyone. That's why a baptism administered by any of these is invalid. It also explains why true, first-century churches do not accept such baptisms. No baptism is valid except one administered by one of the Lord's churches. Those which deserted the teachings of Scripture and split off at some later time to start a new and different type of *church* with a man as its head are not legitimate and cannot administer valid baptisms. Even though he may have been saved and immersed at the time, anyone having been baptized by such an organization needs to be baptized scripturally. Until (1) a believer is baptized (2) in the right manner (3) by a proper authority, God will not view his baptism as valid.

Section Two

It is now time to teach your student that when he is baptized he will become a member of one of the Lord's churches.

A. It is at the point of baptism that God Himself adds one to the church.

   1. Add **Church** to the chart and write **Acts 2:41, 47** under it as shown.

   2. From these Scriptures you can easily show your student that God chooses to add people to His church at the point of baptism. He adds people to His family when they believe on Him as Savior but He only adds them to His church when they publicly identify themselves with Him in baptism.

B. There are a great, great many benefits to those children of God who become members and active participants in one of the Lord's churches.

1. **TEACHER:** Be careful that you do not bog down right here. There are so many good things to be said for being active in the Lord's church. If you try to name them all and turn your student to every reference, you'll be here until tomorrow. Your main objective at this point is to sell your student on how helpful and important the church is in God's program. You want to do enough here to get him into church for it's there that he can be brought to maturity. If he doesn't become active in church, he'll continually languish in unfruitfulness and spiritual barrenness as a child of God.

2. I begin by telling my student that God didn't sit around in heaven and think up church just so we'd have something to do on Sundays. Just as God doesn't need the Bible He doesn't need church. Church, like the Bible, was given because we need it. God knows our needs and what it takes to keep us headed in the right direction, and church is one of those things every child of God needs. He needs the preaching he'll get at church. In church he'll hear preaching and be taught the Word of God. Without this input, the world will capture his attention and take his eyes off the way of God. He will inevitably begin to wander away from God and into trouble. He will find himself embracing the attitudes and philosophies of the world. Believers need the fellowship of people of like mind and they get it at church. Too much time with only unsaved people can influence anyone in the wrong direction. Also believers need to be a part of the ministry of the Lord's church. Through many ministries churches reach out to people who are yet unsaved and to believers who are saved but backslidden. As a part of the Lord's church your student can become a part of a worldwide missionary ministry. Another benefit of active church affiliation is worship. There is no way to duplicate the spiritually uplifting and inspiring atmosphere which prevails in a church service when God's people get together to worship God in prayers, singing, giving, preaching and the Lord's Supper. Watching a church service on T.V. does not produce the same effect. Christ is the head of His church and the church is called His body. He meets with the church and has given the task of carrying on His work on earth to His church corporately. There is so much to be said for the

church. If your student does not become an active member of one of the Lord's churches, he will be cheating himself.

C. Every child of God is commanded to be an active part of one of the Lord's churches.

1. **Ephesians 3:21** (add to chart) says He wants all glory that comes to Him to come through His church. If work for God is going to count, it must be done through a church.

2. Add **Hebrews 10:24-25** to the chart and have your student see it. This passage plainly says God's children ought not to forsake regular assembly with the Lord's church.

Section Three

At this point teach your student that God wants him to worship Him. (Add **Worship** to the chart.)

A. Explain that one of the things we do as a part of the Lord's church is worship God.

1. We do it as we sing. (Add **Sing** to chart.) Singing expresses the emotions and adoration of our hearts for God. An excellent reference for this is Colossians 3:16.

2. We worship in the church by giving. (Add **Give** to the chart.) Giving expresses our realization that God is the owner and we are only stewards of material things. A reference is 1 Corinthians 16:2.

3. We worship in the church by praying. (Add **Pray** to the chart.) Prayer is asking from God. It also acknowledges our subjection to and need of Him. A reference is Ephesians 6:18.

4. We worship in the church by preaching. (Add **Preach** to the chart.) Preaching is God's primary way of setting forth the Word of truth. A reference is 1 Corinthians 1:21.

5. We also worship God in church with the **Lord's Supper.** (Add to the chart.) The Lord's Supper is a recognition that our salvation and hope are solely because of Christ who gave His body and blood for us. A reference is 1 Corinthians 11:23-33.

TEACHER: You can elaborate on these as much or as little as time will allow and you feel the given situation demands. It is certain that you cannot cover them with much detail. Be careful that you do not allow yourself to become too detailed and technical. As your student grows he'll get more of this through the teaching ministry of the church. Time limits you in six one-hour lessons.

B. Next teach your student that there are two basic requirements for true worship of God. (Add **John 4:23-24** to the chart and have your student turn there.)

   1. God seeks people to worship Him *"in spirit."* That means the attitude and motive in worship must be right. Remember the section of study on *"love."* It is to be the only true motive for anything we do in the work of God. Merely going through the motions of worship when our heart is not there is vain worship. The biggest offering, the greatest song, the finest prayer, the most powerful sermon or a moving Lord's Supper when the heart is not humbly in tune with God is vain.

   2. God also seeks people to worship Him *"in truth."* It is not enough to be sincere, earnest and have a good spirit about our worship of God. We are not at liberty to do merely what we feel like doing and have it blessed of God. God has prescribed that certain things be done in a certain way. For example, when it's time to assemble in worship we cannot skip it in favor of our own fireside service at home or the lakeside and expect God will accept our worship. When we worship in singing, our songs must tell the truth. There's a right amount to give and a right place to give it. Teach your student that one of the responsibilities of the leadership of the Lord's church is to teach people how to properly worship God in truth.

Section Four

Teach your student that God also wants His children to serve Him. (Add **Service** to the chart.)

A. Tell your student to be careful not to confuse service with worship.

1. Many people think because they are faithful to go to church and worship that they are *serving* God. Worship is adoration and praise to God. Service is active engagement in activities that enhance the cause of Christ and which bring honor and glory to Him. A person may very well be faithful to the worship times of the church and yet never serve God. Worship encourages service but they are not one and the same.

2. In a general sense service is what one does before and after the formal worship of God. Yes, there are service capacities in a church. One may serve as a deacon, a teacher or in a ministry like the bus ministry, printing ministry or the treasury. In fact there are many, many places to serve in a good church.

   However church service is just one part of the bigger service picture. Being a Christian is not a Sunday-only proposition. Wherever we are our lives are to represent and serve God well every day. We're to be good employees every day. Whether or not we realize it we represent and are serving (or not serving) God all day every day. We're to be serving mates, parents, employees and citizens. Every opportunity we have to stand up for Jesus in word or deed is an opportunity to serve Him. People are coming into our lives every day. God views our responses to them as personal, just as though we had treated Him the way we treated them.

   TEACHER: Write **Matthew 25:31-40** on the chart and read it to your student. It is sobering indeed. Particularly note verse 40. Jesus views our treatment of those around us as treatment of Him personally. Yes, teach your student to serve God. Every day!

B. *TEACHER:* Show your student that since he is now saved serving God is to be his life's work.

   1. Add **Ephesians 2:10** to the chart and read or quote it. Teach your student to ever be on the lookout for opportunities to do good works in serving God.

   2. A good way to wrap up this point, which basically concludes the new material of these lessons, is to encourage your student to begin doing exactly what you are doing.

Encourage him to get into a training course and learn this material so that he can begin teaching others even as you have taught him. Remind him that there are many out there who need it, many more than you can possibly teach personally. This work needs help, more teachers. In fact point out to him that there are doubtless people who would let him teach them but who would never allow you to teach them. This is also a good time to ask him if he knows of someone with whom he could set up these lessons. Tell him you'll be glad to teach them. This will help you get new prospects to teach while providing an opportunity for you to start training your student to become a teacher.

Section Five

Finally tell your student that you would like to conclude the six lessons by pointing out the progressive nature of the truths involved in the lessons.

TEACHER: Look at the big arrow on the chart at the end of this chapter. Draw it on to your chart beginning at the point (not the tail) of the arrow. You are going to draw the arrow onto the sheet in reverse order of the way you taught the material. This will serve as your comprehensive review of the six lessons.

As you draw the arrow onto the chart explain it something like this. Every child of God ought to *serve* God (add your arrow point); but no child of God will be in any position to serve God, nor will he long to do so, who does not first *worship* God. (Extend your arrow shaft through *worship*.) Furthermore no one is qualified to worship God who is not a part of one of the Lord's churches. Worship is to be done in the church. (The arrow shaft now goes through *church*.) However no one is part of one of the Lord's churches until he is baptized. (Extend the arrow shaft now through *baptism*.) Everyone who is baptized should do so because he *loves* God and *wants to* be baptized, not because he *has to* be baptized. (Extend the arrow shaft through *love*.) Point out that no one who doesn't learn to walk in *fellowship* with God is going to be successful in any of this. (Continue the arrow shaft now upward through *fellowship*.) Point out that there is no way to be in fellowship with God until *relationship* is first established with Him. (The arrow shaft now goes to *relationship*.) Next point out that all who would have relationship with God must come by way of the cross of Jesus Christ. (The arrow shaft now passes through *the cross*.) Furthermore no one will come to Jesus Christ until he recognizes himself to be a lost, hopeless sinner, unable to save himself. (At this point run the arrow shaft downward through *the "X'd" out good works section* and on upward to the top of the left hand column as shown. Add the feathers at the rear of the arrow.) Finally you can say to your student that there is a definite progressive order involved in God's truth. With that you should again encourage him to become a part of the program of sharing these truths with others.

Let your student know that you care and that you are available to help him in his new Christian walk. Give him contact information. Help him plug-in to your church. Introduce him to others who can become a part of his growth team. Stay in his life. Let him know that you will be calling and praying for him. I strongly recommend that you enlist him in *Basic Discipleship* which is a companion follow-up course to *Basic Bible Truths*. The material is available at www.lesterhutson.org.

AS YOU LEAVE:

1. Thank your student for giving you the opportunity to share these precious truths with him.

2. Tell him you look forward to working with him in the church in the days ahead. Assure him you will do everything you can to help him grow in the Lord.

3. Ask if there are any questions you might clear up before you leave.

4. Lead in prayer thanking God for the privilege you've had to share these truths and asking His blessings upon the effort put forth and upon this home.

5. Rise up and make your way to the door with a warm expression of your love.

Lesson Six

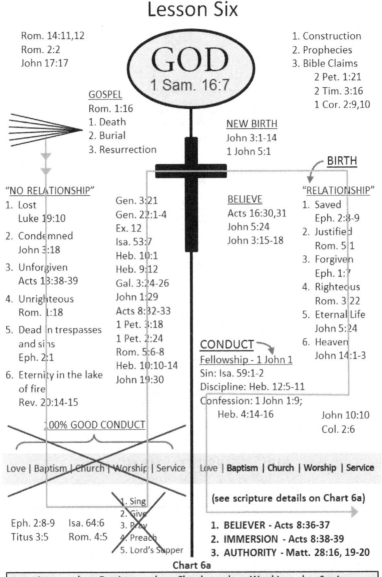

Rom. 14:11,12
Rom. 2:2
John 17:17

GOD
1 Sam. 16:7

1. Construction
2. Prophecies
3. Bible Claims
   2 Pet. 1:21
   2 Tim. 3:16
   1 Cor. 2:9,10

GOSPEL
Rom. 1:16
1. Death
2. Burial
3. Resurrection

NEW BIRTH
John 3:1-14
1 John 5:1

BIRTH

"NO RELATIONSHIP"
1. Lost
   Luke 19:10
2. Condemned
   John 3:18
3. Unforgiven
   Acts 13:38-39
4. Unrighteous
   Rom. 1:18
5. Dead in trespasses
   and sins
   Eph. 2:1
6. Eternity in the lake
   of fire
   Rev. 20:14-15

Gen. 3:21
Gen. 22:1-4
Ex. 12
Isa. 53:7
Heb. 10:1
Heb. 9:12
Gal. 3:24-26
John 1:29
Acts 8:32-33
1 Pet. 3:18
1 Pet. 2:24
Rom. 5:6-8
Heb. 10:10-14
John 19:30

BELIEVE
Acts 16:30,31
John 5:24
John 3:15-18

"RELATIONSHIP"
1. Saved
   Eph. 2:8-9
2. Justified
   Rom. 5:1
3. Forgiven
   Eph. 1:7
4. Righteous
   Rom. 3:22
5. Eternal Life
   John 5:24
6. Heaven
   John 14:1-3

CONDUCT
Fellowship - 1 John 1
Sin: Isa. 59:1-2
Discipline: Heb. 12:5-11
Confession: 1 John 1:9;
   Heb. 4:14-16

John 10:10
Col. 2:6

100% GOOD CONDUCT

Love | Baptism | Church | Worship | Service

Love | **Baptism** | **Church** | **Worship** | **Service**

(see scripture details on Chart 6a)

Eph. 2:8-9   Isa. 64:6
Titus 3:5   Rom. 4:5

1. Sing
2. Give
3. Pray
4. Preach
5. Lord's Supper

1. **BELIEVER** - Acts 8:36-37
2. **IMMERSION** - Acts 8:38-39
3. **AUTHORITY** - Matt. 28:16, 19-20

Chart 6a

Love		Baptism		Church		Worship	Service
1 Peter 4:8		Acts 2:41		Acts 2:41,47		1. Sing	Matt. 25:31-40
2 Cor. 5:14		Acts 16:33		Eph. 3:21		2. Give	Eph. 2:10
1 Cor. 13:1-3		"Picture of		Heb. 10:24-25		3. Pray	
1 Cor. 10:31		the Gospel"				4. Preach	
		Rom. 6:4-5				5. Lord's Supper	
						John 4:23-24	

STUDY SHEET & LESSON PLAN

LESSON SIX

TITLE

"Worshipping and Serving God as a Part of One of His Churches"

THOUGHT

A CERTAIN TYPE OF CONDUCT IS NECESSARY TO A CONTINUING FELLOWSHIP WITH GOD AND FOR EFFECTIVENESS IN HIS WORK.

APPLICATION

Cause the student to realize that in order to please God and stay in fellowship with Him proper baptism, church membership, worship and service are necessary. Explain in some detail what these activities are.

BIBLE VERSES TO MEMORIZE

Acts 2:41 *"Then they that gladly received his word were baptized: and the same day there were added unto them about three thousand souls."*

Ephesians 3:21 *"Unto him be glory in the church by Christ Jesus throughout all ages, world without end. Amen."*

Hebrews 10:24-25 *"And let us consider one another to provoke unto love and to good works: Not forsaking the assembling of ourselves together, as the manner of some is; but exhorting one another: and so much the more, as ye see the day approaching."*

126

John 4:23-24 *"But the hour cometh, and now is, when the true worshippers shall worship the Father in spirit and truth: for the Father seeketh such to worship him. God is a Spirit: and they that worship him must worship him in spirit and in truth."*

Ephesians 2:10 *"For we are his workmanship, created in Christ Jesus unto good works, which God hath before ordained that we should walk in them."*

OUTLINE

LESSON SIX

I. **A look at a valid baptism.**

    A. The first act of conduct for a child of God. **Acts 2:41, Acts 16:33, Romans 6:4-5.** It is a **Picture of the Gospel.**

    B. Three requirements of God for a valid baptism.

    ILLUSTRATE HERE. The notarization of legal documents.

        1. The candidate must be a **BELIEVER. Acts 8:36-37**

        2. The method must be **IMMERSION. Acts 8:38-39**

        3. The baptism must be by the **AUTHORITY** of a church like Jesus Christ built. **Matthew 28:16, 19-20, 1 Corinthians 12:28, Matthew 16:18**

        TRANSITION THOUGHT: By the proper authority, in the right manner, as a believer.

II. **Being a member of one of the Lord's churches. Add Church**

    A. The Lord adds one to the church at the point of baptism. **Acts 2:41, 47.**

    B. Great benefits to God's children who are members of and participants in one of His churches.

    C. We are commanded of God to be an active part of a church. **Ephesians 3:21, Hebrews 10:24-25.**

> *TRANSITION THOUGHT:* Do not forsake regular assembly.

III. **God wants His children to worship Him. Add Worship**

   A. We worship in a church as we (1) **Sing**, (2) **Give**, (3) **Pray**, (4) **Preach** and (5) observe the **Lord's Supper**.

   B. Two basic requirements for true worship. **John 4:23-24**

      1. *"In spirit."*

      2. *"In truth."*

      TRANSITION THOUGHT: Church leadership is responsible to teach believers how to worship in truth.

IV. **God wants His children to give Service to Him. Add Serve**

   A. Service is not to be confused with worship.

      1. Worshipping is not serving.

      2. God views our treatment of others as personal treatment of Him. **Matthew 25:31-40**

   B. Serving God is to be the life work of the children of God. **Ephesians 2:10**

V. **The progressive nature of these truths.**

   Draw the arrow in reverse order to connect each truth with the others.

CONCLUDING THOUGHT: Encourage your student to practice the same work you are doing in reaching others for Christ.

7

SEVEN

How to Present Christ When You Have Only One Opportunity

The lost jailer in Philippi, *"Sirs, what must I do to be saved?"* The Apostle Paul and his co-worker, Silas, *"Believe on the Lord Jesus Christ, and thou shalt be saved."*

Acts 16:30-31

REDEEM THE TIME YOU ARE GIVEN

There will be many times when you will not have six hours to present the gospel message to a lost person. Whenever possible present the Christian case as thoroughly as possible with six complete lessons but never allow even a brief opportunity to escape you. The neighbor on your street may give you only a short encounter. The co-worker where you work may never sit down at a table with you. The chances are slim that you will ever again see the waiter who serves you or the person in the plane seat next to you. Your family member may not agree to six one-hour lessons. Do not fail to do what you can because you don't have ideal conditions or because you do not have enough time to present the case as thoroughly as you wish. In his fables Aesop spoke of Kairos one of the ancient Greek gods. Kairos was thought to be the spirit of opportunity. He was described as completely naked and bald except for one lock of hair coming from his forehead. The idea is that opportunity is always coming toward you (from the future to you.) You must grab it as it comes. Once it has passed it is impossible to grab hold. When you have only one opportunity to present the gospel capitalize immediately. When you pay your waiter, fold your payment inside a gospel tract. (Always carry a supply of good salvation tracts and distribute them freely.) During brief encounters bring up the subject of the brevity of life and the reality of eternity. Let the joy of your own heart show and give your relationship to Christ the credit. Doing so immediately brings up the hope that is in Christ and opens the door to an explanation. Maybe you will get in only a few sentences; you may get 30 minutes. Plant a seed wherever you are even when the opportunity is fleeting. Do what you can with the opportunity provided. There will be times when the most you can do is leave a tract. On other occasions there will be time for only brief conversation. Door-knocking, soul-winning in public places and encounters in a shopping setting often provide only brief windows of opportunity. A medical waiting room, an airline flight or a response to an evangelistic service invitation will likely afford you several minutes or an hour. Each given situation will dictate how much time you have. The key is to take advantage of whatever time you're given. That means being ready: (1) prepared to seize the initiative and bring up the subject and (2) being equipped to present your case by tailoring it to the time afforded.

In the case cited above (Acts 16) Paul and Silas were presented a one-time opportunity to bring the jailer in Philippi to Christ. He asked how to be saved and they answered him *on-the-spot*. No attempt was made to set up home Bible studies. (There is good reason to believe that discipleship follow-up occurred.) Paul and Silas capitalized on the opportunity at hand. Jesus did that with the Samaritan woman, John 4:6-26, Zacchaeus, Luke 19:1-9, Nicodemus, John 3:1-21, and others. Yokefellow, do not let opportunities to bring people to Christ get past you. Bringing souls to Him is our business, our primary reason for being!

KEY ELEMENTS IN THE GOSPEL MESSAGE

The Bible says that *"faith cometh by hearing, and hearing by the word of God,"* Romans 10:17. What truths does a lost person need to hear in order to be saved? Though getting saved is an event, not a process, it is obvious that certain background information is essential. For example, the lost sinner cannot make a decision to believe on Jesus Christ until he knows who Christ is. That lost sinner need not become an expert theologian in order to be saved however there are key elements in the gospel message which lost sinners must grasp. They must be a part of even the shortest presentation.

1. There is a God to whom each of us must ultimately answer.

2. We know God and what He thinks because He has told us in His Word, the Bible.

3. Every one of us has sinned or failed before God.

4. The consequence of our sins is eternal death in the lake of fire.

5. There is nothing any of us can do to rescue ourselves from the consequences of our sins.

6. God loves us in spite of our sins.

7. God loved us enough to send His own Son, Jesus, into this world as a sinless human.

8. Jesus took our sins upon his self and shed His blood in death in our place upon a cross to pay our death penalty once and for all.

9. Jesus, being God in the flesh, rose from the dead after three days and will never die again.

10. Because of what Jesus did for us God can forgive our sins and give us eternal life.

11. The only way to receive the forgiveness and eternal life that is in Jesus Christ is by personal faith, trust or belief in Him. Forgiveness and eternal life are by grace; they are not the result of anything within human merit or power.

12. All who believe in Jesus Christ as personal Savior receive eternal life and are saved forever.

These twelve statements are a summary of the first four lessons in *Basic Bible Truths*. Keep in mind that latent biblical background information varies from person to person. To different degrees those you meet will already be familiar with some of these truths. Some have almost no knowledge of this information; others grew up in a Christian home or some environment that filled them with the truths related to salvation. More or less emphasis can thus be placed here or there as necessary and as time permits.

PRESENTING

LESSON SEVEN

In order to prepare you to present these truths in the most effective way I recommend that you make this *title*, this *thought* and this *application* a part of you. This entire lesson should be a part of you. When you teach the six lessons of *Basic Bible Truths* you are able to study or review ahead of time for each lesson. Not so with spontaneous opportunities. Here you must present the gospel *on-the-spot* with no time to prepare yourself and with no notes. You'll have to present your case strictly from what's in your heart and you will have to tailor it to the need of the person before you within the time available. The Bible says, *"Be ready always to give an answer to every man that asketh you a reason of the hope that is within you with meekness and fear,"* 1 Peter 3:15. May the information that is offered here both equip and motivate you to win souls!

TITLE

"How to Present Christ When You Have Only One Opportunity"

THOUGHT

QUICKLY PRESENT KEY BACKGROUND INFORMATION AND INVITE THE SINNER BEFORE YOU TO TRUST CHRIST BASED ON THE TRUTH YOU PRESENT.

APPLICATION

Your objective is to present sufficient background information to enable the person before you to put his faith in Jesus Christ as his personal Savior and to plead with him to do so.

PRESENTING

Keep flexibility and adaptability in mind. We're talking here of situations where you are almost certain to have only one opportunity to present the gospel and bring this person to Christ. You must (1) read the situation, (2) read the person before you and (3) adapt to the opportunity afforded. Whether it's a brief exchange with a waiter or an extended conversation with someone dropped into your life by God, be grateful for the time you get and make the most of it. This lesson assumes a scenario of approximately 30 to 60 minutes. During this time your task, in the spirit of love and genuine concern, is to establish the key elements of the gospel message as seen above.

Caution: Do not become too detailed. Make your point and keep moving.

There is a good possibility that the person before you already has a fundamental knowledge of the Christian message. Capitalize on that knowledge and do not attempt to teach this person what he already knows. Place your emphasis on what he does not know and on correcting misconceptions. It is most likely that his biggest misconception will have to do with being saved by some form of good behavior and works. Most people have the preconceived misconception that being saved is somehow related to being good. They think going to church, being baptized, saying a prayer or cutting down on sins will get them to heaven. I recommend that you do not start on a misconception or highlight the fact that you are clearing up a misconception. Simply take the *high ground* and stay positive, not negative. Start at the beginning and follow the logical progression of truth inherent in the key elements of the gospel message as set forth above.

Caution: Beware of questions. They can quickly derail you and eat up your time. Some interchange is necessary but you should lead the conversation. When it gets off track bring it back.

Assuming that you have several minutes to talk to a lost person about being saved here is a suggested approach. Note that this approach is designed to move through three necessary stages:

1. It turns attention to the issue of sin, forgiveness and eternal salvation.

2. It presents the key elements of the gospel message.

3. It challenges the lost person to trust Christ as his own personal Savior.

Section One

Turn the conversation to the subject of salvation. You will not win anyone to salvation apart from the gospel message of Jesus Christ. Health, sports, weather and other points of conversation have their place but they do not bring people to salvation. Remember, *"Faith cometh by hearing, and hearing by the word of God,"* Romans 10:17. You must get around to the subject and you don't have much time to do it. Don't waste time; move quickly.

A. If the person before you is a stranger, here are suggested ways for turning the conversation to the subject of salvation.

1. "Hi, I'm (state your name)." After hearing his name say something like, "It's great to be a child of God and know that you have eternal life. The best day of my life was the day I met Jesus Christ as my own personal Savior. Do you know that your sins are forgiven and you have eternal life?"

2. Another popular and good approach is to ask, "If you died today, do you know for sure that you are going to be with God in heaven?" The person's response is to be followed with, "If God were to ask you, 'Why should I let you into My heaven?' what would you say?"

3. Approaches of this sort are almost certain to generate responses.

   a. It is impossible here to give specific answers to each potential response. Your answers and follow-up to whatever response you receive should be natural, spontaneous and from your heart. They should not be canned answers as if you are reciting something by rote. Hearts reach hearts. Answers that come across as artificial and not a part of you tend to turn people away.

   b. The person before you is likely to counter with a response such as, "What makes you think there is a God?" Many will tell you that they are members of some

136

church. A growing number will say they have no use for "organized religion." Still others will challenge that one religion is just as good as any other.

c. It is so very important that you be prepared! The Bible says, *"Study to shew thyself approved unto God, a workman that needeth not to be ashamed, rightly dividing the word of truth,"* 2 Timothy 2:15.

1) A brief, straightforward apologetics-oriented answer may be in order however it must not be long, complicated or too detailed. You do not have much time and usually a simple, short, honest answer is sufficient.

2) Rather than bog down in a lengthy debate at this point I recommend something like this, "We could spend lots of time discussing theology and religion, who is right and who is wrong and get nowhere. But one thing is obvious and certain; one of these days every one of us is going to die. The unavoidable question is, 'Where do we go when we leave here?'"

3) At this point you have accomplished your first objective; you have turned the conversation to the subject of salvation. Furthermore you have set the stage for your second objective which is to present the key elements of the gospel message. Without delay, launch into presenting the gospel message. How to do so is addressed below in the second major section of this outline.

B. If the Lord opens a door for you into the life of a lost person whom you already know, here are suggested ways for turning the conversation to the subject of salvation.

1. Address the person by name and say something like, "(his name), with all my heart I want you to go to heaven when you die and you and I both know that one day you will die."

2. At this point the conversation has been turned to the subject of salvation. Unless the person refuses to let you talk to him the stage is now set for you to launch into a presentation of the gospel message as seen below.

Section Two

Present the key elements of the gospel message.

A. It is not vital that the key elements of the gospel message be presented with the identical language or in the exact order as seen here. It is vital that the sinner grasp the heart of the gospel message. He should:

1. See himself as a guilty before God and come to the realization that the consequence of his sin is eternal separation from God in the lake of fire.

2. See that he is absolutely powerless to save himself.

3. See Christ alone as his hope and realize that Christ can and will save him upon the strength of His own redemptive work for sinners: His own blood which He shed when He died, was buried and rose again.

4. See that the work of Christ will become personally his only when he trusts Him or believes on Him as his own personal Savior. The decision to abandon all other hope and come in his heart to Jesus Christ for forgiveness of sins and eternal life is made in the heart and it must be real and genuine. This is the essence of repentance toward God and faith toward the Lord Jesus Christ as mentioned in Acts 20:21 and it brings about forgiveness of sins and eternal life. When a person comes to this point of faith in his heart, he is saved on the spot.

B. Here is the approach that I have used many times.

1. Remember the unavoidable question that you have posed, "Where do we go when we leave here?" Follow this question with a line of thought such as this.

   a. All persons who die without Christ as their personal Savior go to the lake of fire, not heaven.

   b. That's because all people are sinners. The Bible which God claims to be His word says, *"All have sinned, and come short of the glory of God,"* Romans 3:23. Every one of us knows we are a sinner.

138

   c. Sin has eternal consequences. Romans 6:23 says, *"The wages of sin is death."* Yes. Sin demands the eternal death penalty, eternity in the lake of fire.

   d. The fact is that there is not one thing either of us can do about the condemnation of sin that is upon us. Forgiveness of sins and eternal life do not come by merit; they come by grace or the unmerited favor of God. Salvation comes by what God has done for us, not by what we can do for ourselves or for Him. The Bible says, *"For by grace are ye saved through faith; and that not of yourselves; it is the gift of God,"* Ephesians 2:8. Joining a church, any church, cannot save you. Neither can baptism, a prayer or any good work you can do.

   e. However God can save you and He wants to do it. John 3:16 says He loved sinners (including you) enough to send His own Son into this world to die on the cross in their place. Listen to the Bible say it, *"when we were yet without strength, in due time Christ died for the ungodly,"* Romans 5:6. Jesus Christ, who was God in a human body, was sinless. Yet, He *"bare our sins in his own body on the tree, that we, being dead to sins, should live unto righteousness,"* 1 Peter 2:24. He died for our sins, He was buried in a tomb, but three days later He rose from the dead. That work of God on our behalf is called the gospel or good news of Christ and it's upon the strength of that work that God can save us from the awful penalty of sin. The Bible says, *"For I am not ashamed of the gospel of Christ: for it is the power of God unto salvation to every one that believeth,"* Romans 1:16.

   f. For you to be saved you must accept Christ's work on your behalf. The only way to accept His work is by faith in Him. It's a matter of trust, faith, belief in Him. The Bible says, *"He that believeth on the Son hath everlasting life: and he that believeth not the Son shall not see life; but the wrath of God abideth on him,"* John 3:36. To be saved you must trust Christ as your very own personal Savior. The Bible promises, *"Believe on the Lord Jesus Christ, and thou shalt be saved,"* Acts 16:31.

2. It is now time to challenge this lost person to trust Christ.

Section Three

Challenge the lost person to trust Christ as his own personal Savior.

A. With compassion and intensity I ask the person before me, "Will you right now trust Jesus Christ as your own personal Savior?"

    1. On the spot some will say, "Yes." Others will hesitate. When they do I usually say, "I am going to wait here and give you time to take care of this most important matter."

    2. When a person acknowledges that he has trusted Christ I rejoice with him and offer a prayer of thanksgiving.

    3. Before parting company:

        a. Capture the name and contact information of this person.

        b. Give him your name and contact information in writing.

        c. Carry a supply of tracts. Give one to this new believer.

        d. Instruct him to find a church that is committed to the Bible where he can find further instructions about following Christ.

        e. Promise to send him information that will help him on his new spiritual journey.

B. When the person with whom I am dealing continues to remain tentative or uncertain I bring out a sheet of paper.

    1. I use the paper to present a condensed version of the John 3:36 chart as seen in lesson four of this series. This exercise proves especially beneficial in cases where a person thinks maybe he is saved but is not sure.

    2. I place the sheet on a flat surface and quickly write **John 3:36** along with the words, *"He that believeth on the Son hath everlasting life."*

    3. I point out that this is God's promise that all believers have everlasting life. That's another way of saying they are saved.

4. One at a time, in progressive order, I list three questions:

   a. **Are you saved?**

   b. **How were you saved?**

   c. **When were you saved?**

5. I then draw the lifeline and ask this person to tell me when it happened (when he was saved).

   a. When a person can't give a firm answer I ask him to trust Christ now.

   b. Once he trusts Christ, I write the date and time on the chart and give the paper to him.

   c. If he does not trust Christ, I plead with him to do so without delay. I give him my contact information and assure him that I stand ready to offer further help. I get his contact information and ask him to stay in touch. I also make sure he gets a sound gospel tract.

Whenever possible follow through on this person whom God has placed in your life.

1. Stay in contact.

2. If the person didn't get saved, keep trying. Write, call and do all you can to reach him.

3. For those who get saved:

   a. Send discipleship information.

   b. Help him locate a good church.

   c. Contact the pastor of that church, explain what has happened and ask follow-up help for this new believer.

   d. Pray for him.

BIBLE VERSES TO MEMORIZE

Please understand that these verses should become a part of you. You should master them and always have them at ready recall. Opportunity usually presents itself unexpectedly. When it does you are not likely to have time to refresh yourself on the key verses you will need to make a gospel presentation. Work to commit them to your heart and they will serve you well when the door of opportunity suddenly swings open.

Romans 3:23 *"For all have sinned, and come short of the glory of God."*

Romans 6:23 *"The wages of sin is death."*

Ephesians 2:8 *"For by grace are ye saved through faith; and that not of yourselves; it is the gift of God."*

John 3:16 *"For God so loved the world, that he gave his only begotten Son, that whosoever believeth in him should not perish, but have everlasting life."*

Romans 5:6 *"For when we were yet without strength, in due time, Christ died for the ungodly."*

1 Peter 2:24 *"Who his own self bare our sins in his own body on the tree, that we, being dead to sins, should live unto righteousness."*

Romans 1:16 *"For I am not ashamed of the gospel of Christ: for it is the power of God unto salvation to every one that believeth."*

Acts 16:30-31 *"Sirs, what must I do to be saved? And they said, Believe on the Lord Jesus Christ, and thou shalt be saved."*

John 3:36 *"He that believeth on the Son hath everlasting life: and he that believeth not the Son shall not see life; but the wrath of God abideth on him."*

8

EIGHT

General Information
and Teaching Techniques

The intent of this chapter is to further explain the concept of the *Basic Bible Truths Home Bible Studies Course* and to enable you to more effectively teach this material.

THE CONCEPT OF BASIC BIBLE TRUTHS

Though insight into this concept is inherent throughout this *Teacher's Manual* let me now enunciate what the **Basic Bible Truths** *Home Bible Studies Ministry* is. The basic intent in *Basic Bible Truths* is to present six one-hour lessons to a student at a mutually acceptable time over a six-week period. The teaching is usually more effective when you teach one person, couple or family at a time. Additional people in the group often inhibit other students causing them to withhold their true feelings and questions for fear of what their friends or neighbors might think. The six lessons are normally presented in the student's home around the dining room table or some other table with a flat writing surface where the chart can be laid out along with the Bible. Sometimes it is advantageous to teach the lessons at a third location such as the church facilities where a baby sitter can be made available.

Because the nature of the material being presented is simple, yet very weighty and profound, six one-hour lessons seem to produce better results than an effort to present all of this material in one or two longer teaching sessions. Allowing a week between each of the one-hour lessons allows time for the student to digest and assimilate the material in an orderly manner. Presentation of too much of this material at a time can overtax the student's comprehension and understanding and result in confusion.

An agreement by a student to take the six-lesson course sets up a definite appointment in which your student knows you are coming and why you are coming. A great percentage of the uncertainty that prevails in customary visitation is eliminated. Fruitless hours spent in finding no one home are also avoided. By teaching a single person (or family) in his home or at some other private location an informal atmosphere is created. That is very conducive to the teaching-learning effort.

The actual material to be taught, which is contained in the first six chapters of this *Teacher's Manual*, is basic and systematic. The basics or fundamentals of Christianity are set forth and they are set forth in a cohesive, systematic, biblical progression. One point leads to another systematically building a clear overview of Christianity. I call it *"the big picture."*

In a very real sense with *Basic Bible Truths* you are getting a student to agree to hear the case of Christianity. He agrees to listen with concentration and you agree to present in a systematic and scholarly way the case of Christianity as set forth in the Bible. It is a sad reality that most people have never really stopped long enough to hear our Christian case. They've heard bits and pieces but they've never comprehended *the big picture*. It is even sadder to say that most believers do not know how to present well, in a biblically logical and structured way, the great case we have. They do not know where to start or where to end or what should be presented second or third or tenth. We have the greatest case there is and once people truly hear and see it they find it profoundly revolutionary. *Basic Bible Truths* is simply a forum or vehicle by which any believer, who is serious about getting into the lives of others with the message of Christ, can clearly and systematically present the Christian case to a student who is willing to listen. That's really all *Basic Bible Truths* is. It is neither a gimmick nor a sophisticated method of tricking someone into a *decision*. It is simply presenting the Christian case to one willing to hear it.

AN EVANGELISM AND A DISCIPLESHIP TOOL

Basic Bible Truths is both a discipleship as well as an evangelism tool. The first four lessons are primarily evangelistic while the final two are primarily discipleship oriented. However the material of lessons one through four is the basis or groundwork of true discipleship. Thus even the first four lessons pave the way for true discipleship.

As an evangelism-discipleship tool, *Basic Bible Truths* is designed to counter two major and very common problems plaguing Christianity. One is empty professions of faith. An alarming number who are *won to Christ* in quick sessions in the home, on street corners or during institutional evangelistic efforts do not *follow through*. Only God knows the heart but time indicates their professions to be false or empty. There is little or no fruit or evidence to indicate that the profession was genuine. Furthermore many who now have a good testimony and are living for the Lord will look back to a point at which they made an *empty profession of faith* in Christ. *Basic Bible Truths* is not a guarantee that all who take the course and who profess Christ as Savior are truly saved. Empty professions can result from these lessons but the thoroughness of this approach has a proven record of reducing the empty profession rate and insuring a greater number of true conversions.

The second problem addressed by the *Basic Bible Truths* approach is *the failure of new converts to grow to maturity*. So many new believers get caught up in the cares of the world or fall to false doctrine. They lack basic grounding in the Christian faith. *Basic Bible Truths* alone will not prevent that but it does provide a strong base from which to build. This approach gives a good initial push in the right direction. Coupled with a good new member growth program in a church, *Basic Bible Truths* can help solidify new converts and bring them to stability and spiritual maturity.

145

THE CHART AND TEACHING OUTLINES

As the lessons are being taught an illustration chart should be developed. The chart builds throughout the six lessons. Some material is placed on the chart during lesson one. More material is added during lessons two through six. At the end of each lesson leave the chart in the custody of your student. It serves as a good reference and review sheet for him. As you begin the next lesson he's to bring out the chart and you build on it. You do not start a new chart each lesson unless your student loses the initial chart.

At the end of each of the six lessons, which are written out in full detail in this *Teacher's Manual*, you will see the chart as it should look on your sheet when you complete that given lesson. When you go to teach lesson one take a large blank sheet of paper. Develop your chart on it as shown here in your *Teacher's Manual*.

You will also notice a teaching outline at the end of each of the six lessons of this *Teacher's Manual*. These outlines correspond with the six fully written lessons. The idea is for YOU as a teacher to first master the material in the fully written lessons. The brief outline is to serve as a brief guide and reminder sheet to you as you actually teach the lesson. After a while you probably won't need the outline as you will have it committed to heart.

Note also that certain words in the written lessons and in the outlines are in bold type. All of these, except the major Roman numeral points, are to be added to the chart at the appropriate time. They are in bold type to remind you that this is the time to add that word or phrase to the chart.

DUPLICATE PAGES

On the www.lesterhutson.org website (in the *Products > Free Resources* section), you will find duplicate pages of each (1) *Study sheet and lesson plan*, (2) *chart* and (3) *outline*. These pages are there for you to print out and take with you when you go to teach. In so doing you will not destroy your *Teacher's Manual*. These pages are designed to fit right inside the cover of an average-sized Bible.

HOW TO SET UP THE BIBLE CLASSES

For most people setting up the Bible classes is the hardest part. Once the setup is made those who give themselves to mastering this material can actually teach the lessons without too much difficulty but getting a course set up seems illusive.

One of the reasons this part is so hard for most people is their tentative and uncertain approach to making the setup. They seem nervous and uncertain about setting up the course. That makes the prospective student nervous and uncertain about taking the course. Thus those who would set up these lessons should have a very positive and relaxed approach, not arrogant or pushy, but positive.

Certainty and confidence in how you are going to go about setting up the course tends to gender effectiveness in your approach. Those who would teach these lessons should master this approach. You will not be able to teach these lessons, if you never learn to set up the course.

Prospective students are everywhere. They are old and young, rich and poor, educated and uneducated. They are Baptists, Catholics, Church of Christ, Lutherans and all the rest. They work with you, live in your neighborhood and are kin to you. Whether you are on formal *visitation*, at work, at any social gathering or elsewhere, **you should be ever watching** for a Bible class prospect. You will encounter some who are so negative they will not agree to take the course. You'll also see some whose hearts are receptive. They may not know what they need but they know they have a need. They may be going through rough roads in life. Sin has really given them a beating. They need a change and they know it. Mixed marriages offer prime prospects. Those who have been married very long know they have a problem and need to get together in their spiritual lives. Many feel convicted that there is no spiritual involvement in their lives. They know they need it and they know they owe it to their kids. Many are just *nominal* church people. They may be lost or they may be saved; they aren't sure just where they stand. In either case they need these lessons. (Don't be afraid to set up these lessons with a person who is regular in church even one who claims to be saved. If he is saved, these lessons will strengthen and revive him. If he isn't saved, these lessons will make that fact painfully clear and probably result in his salvation. In either case your time will be well invested.)

When you encounter one who you think needs these lessons and who seems to show some measure of openness and receptiveness, I suggest that you follow this five-step approach. (You can also use this same approach on those who do not seem to be receptive. The worst they can do is turn down your offer. Even if they refuse the offer has been made and the door is open should they have a change of mind.)

The following five-step approach to setting up the lessons is not the only way. It is just one way; it is simply the approach I have personally found to be most effective. If you can do it better, more power to you. If you aren't having much success with your way, try this way.

Step one is to establish a friendly atmosphere with your prospect. Talk about general things for four or five minutes, maybe even ten minutes. Find a common denominator of interest. The main objective here is to let this prospective student know you are interested in him and what's happening in his life. You want to be a friend and the prospect is seeing that you are real and *touchable* in a spiritual sense. You are not some pharisaical judge who has come to look down your nose at him or to ram something down his throat.

Step two is to bring the conversation around to spiritual matters. Except in rare occasions, I recommend that you do not make it too heavy. Ask a question like, "Where have you been going to church?" I say something like, "Tell me about your spiritual background and where you've gone to church. Have you visited a church since you moved here?" (Naturally, this part must be adapted to the given situation. Obviously you wouldn't ask these questions to one you've known for a long time or to a family member. To that kind of person I'd say, "You know that we've known each other for a long time and I've never gotten to tell you this story that is so beautiful and precious to me. I'm sorry about that. Would you do me a big favor and agree to give me one hour a week for six weeks to just hear my case. I promise I won't preach to you or put any kind of pressure on you. I won't argue or condemn you, if you don't agree. I am asking you to help me clear my conscience by hearing my story. It would be a big, big favor to me and would mean more to me than I could ever express to you.")

TEACHER: You are actually skipping step two in this case, and plunging right into steps three and four.

148

Once you have the subject around to his spiritual life **step three** is to ask if he's ever had a systematic short course on what Baptists are and what they believe. It will be a rare day when you run across anyone, Baptist or otherwise, who has. I ask something like, "Has anyone ever sat down with you and taught you in a systematic, scholarly way a short course which presents the overall picture of what the Bible teaches and why we believe what we believe?"

Once you get an answer to the question of step three, which will almost always be "No" move right into **step four**. You offer to teach this person such a course. You explain that you have a short course of six one-hour lessons which presents *the big picture* of Christianity and explains why we believe the things we do. You explain that these lessons are systematic with each point building and developing upon the previous point. You explain that they are informal and that no pressure will be exerted by you to get this person to make a decision of any sort. Explain that this is simply a setting forth of our case and any decision this person might make would be strictly on his own. Explain that in the lessons there will be opportunities for him to ask questions related to the material being taught. Explain that you would come right to the home each week at an appointed time and teach the lessons right at the kitchen table using the Bible as your textbook. You then say something like, "Would you let me come and teach these lessons to you?"

If you get an affirmative answer, move to **step five**. Here is where you firm up the specific time and the starting date. When the person says "Yes" in step four, you respond with something like, "How about Tuesday nights at 7:30 p.m.?" If that's not an acceptable time, keep suggesting until a time is reached. You might even ask, "What would be a good time for you?" Once the time is established, set the starting date. I say something like, "Let's start next Tuesday night." Once the starting time is agreed make your departure assuring him you are looking forward to the privilege of teaching him and that you will be there at the appointed time.

At the appointed time go as you said you would. I do not call ahead; I just go. It's much easier for an uncertain student to back out on you over the phone than it is with you standing at his door. Once you are there and get through lesson one many of his fears will be resolved and he'll begin to look forward to your coming. However he'll probably be uneasy until after lesson one.

At step four sometimes a prospect will be hesitant or say "No." If he says "No," don't be offended. Tell him the offer still stands. Leave your contact information and ask him to call you, if he changes his mind. If he is hesitant, explain more about the lessons as to how simple and non-pressured they are. Then ask again. If he wants a little time to think it over, say that you understand and will check again in a few days. By all means do check back. If he puts you off, he usually won't let you teach, but he may. Even if he doesn't, checking back will be a very positive and impressive gesture to him.

SPECIAL NOTES IN TEACHING THE LESSONS

Always bear in mind that **you have an appointment**. Do not take it for granted. Your student knows you promised to come and will be expecting you. To fail to keep the appointment, without proper communications, will destroy the student's confidence in you. If something comes up so that you can't keep the appointment, notify your student as far in advance as possible. I usually exchange phone numbers with the student and ask him to call me, if an extenuating circumstance arises.

Also you agreed to teach a specific curriculum within a specific six week, one hour per week, time frame. Stay with that promise. When you arrive for the lessons be friendly, but don't delay getting to the teaching table and getting right into the material. Your student is expecting it.

When going to teach, **be fresh** with your material. It's good to read again the chapter which you are about to teach. Look up the Scriptures so they will be fresh in your mind. If you need it, take the lesson outline for reference use as you teach. Don't let yourself get stale. The message is too important.

This material is flexible. The basics should be presented in each lesson but the applications and particular emphasis will vary with every student. Do not become a mechanical parrot or robot just spitting out academic information. Be sensitive to the specific needs and background of your student. Chances are that no two lessons will be or should be presented exactly the same. Some will need more Scriptures or more illustrations in a given area than others. Be flexible. Read your student. Meet his needs.

Be careful to **stick to your basic lesson plan**. You can't teach the whole Bible in six weeks. No one is capable. If you deviate very much, you will never get through the material. Your student will never see *the big picture*. Also do not try to be too fancy and *deep*. This is not a forum for you to show off how smart and crafty you are with the Bible. This is a forum for you to get the great truths of Christ across to one who desperately needs them.

TEACHING PITFALLS WHICH CAN DERAIL YOU

As you teach certain bad habits can completely destroy your effectiveness. Many fall into these mistakes without realizing the consequences. When you teach avoid these mistakes.

Failure to do what you promised

Failure to do what you promised makes a liar out of you while destroying your integrity and the trust of your student for you. Therefore, be on time. Quit when you said you would. (Stay longer only if the student is insisting that you do so.) Cover all the material you said you'd cover.

Running down other religions

When you run down another religion you make that religion an *underdog*. The natural tendency of most people is to come to the defense of an *underdog*. When you allow this to happen, you put your student on the defensive and pit yourself against your student. That ruins your effectiveness.

This is not to say that you should avoid the subject of other religions. To the contrary you should be willing to honestly discuss them but always in a way that shows why they are in error. Once you present the facts properly and a false religion is exposed by the facts, your student will generally see it for himself and be in agreement with you. That will never be the case, if you launch a belligerent and nasty attack on that religion. In such cases even the truth you present will usually be rejected.

Wandering in answer to excessive and impertinent questions

A person can ask more questions in five minutes than you can answer in an hour. You should answer pertinent questions by your student but only pertinent questions. If your student starts into unrelated questions, in a polite and nice way ask him to limit his questions to the subject matter being presented. Remind him that you didn't come to teach the whole Bible but rather to present a basic overview. Tell him you will never accomplish that unless you stay pretty close to the material to be presented. Tell him that you might be willing to come back for a seventh session to answer general questions.

Sometimes students will ask questions which will automatically be answered as the lessons progress. In such cases explain that an answer is coming in a later lesson and that at that future point your answer will mean much more in light of the material he will have heard. I usually give a brief capsule answer at the time of the question and tell my student that the answer will be much clearer as the lessons develop.

By all means don't try to answer a question when you don't know. Admit that you do not have all the answers. Let him know that you are also still learning but that you have learned some things of which you are very sure. That is what you are here to teach.

Questions can derail you quicker than almost any other thing. Be careful how you handle them.

Pressuring your student

People have a tendency to back up when they feel they are being forced or pressured into something against their will.

TEACHER: Lead your student; don't drive him. Let him see it for himself and let his decisions be real and genuine, not decisions made under duress or to get you *off his back*. False professions contribute nothing to the cause of Christ.

Failure to remember that you are the invited guest

Do not become too familiar and forward in your student's home. You are the guest. Take charge of the lessons but not the home. If you need water, restroom privileges or other needs, ask. Do not assume.

Burning the bridge behind you

Regardless of what develops endeavor to keep the communication lines and door open for some later person to get into the life of this student. Do not assume that because you can't reach him no one can. If you keep the heart's door open, someone else may later pick up where you leave off and reach this individual.

GREEN LIGHTS AND RED LIGHTS

As you teach learn to recognize what I call *red lights* and do not proceed until you get a *green light*. By a *red light* I mean that in one way or another you have lost your student's attention or have come to a place where proceeding immediately would be either unwise or hazardous. In such cases it is important to wait for a change in the situation. The four most common *red lights* are:

Lost student attention

Crying or other action by a child, the phone ringing, a roach on the wall and a myriad of other things can divert your student's attention away from what you are teaching. The student loses his concentration. Once this happens it is useless for you to proceed with new material especially in view of the fact that so much of this material builds upon previous points. Watch your student. You can generally tell when he is paying attention. When he is not, stop moving forward and seek to regain attention. Sometimes calling his name, a side story, asking for a drink of water or some other such device will regain your student's attention.

Student leaving the room

This often happens when you are teaching more than one student. If one leaves the room for the restroom, to tend a child, to answer the phone or for some other reason, wait until he returns. Tell your student you'll wait for him. It's a good time for a drink of water, to update the chart or to review your other student. Sometimes I use this time to talk about some item of common interest.

Student does not understand

This is progressive information much of which depends upon previously understood concepts. As surely as your student does not understand one of the concepts that blank in understanding will tend to weaken or undermine later conclusions. Watch for questioning or blank looks on the face of your student. Ask him occasionally if he has a question. If you perceive that he does not understand, stop forward movement and help him grasp what he has missed. Explain it a different way. Add an additional Scripture. Do not ignore a gap in his understanding. Clear it before proceeding.

Heading for a direct confrontation

All a direct confrontation will do is alienate your student and possibly close the door of his heart forever. Once you see this *red light* slow down and alter your course. Try a new approach. Sometimes you may have to let the issue cool and approach it from a different angle at a different time. Don't allow yourself to get in a fight. It will gender no good, only harm.

9

NINE

Basic Bible Truths Training

Explanation given at first meeting of level one training

Section One

Begin with a full explanation of what *Basic Bible Truths* is.

A. It is a plan in which six one-hour Bible lessons are taught to an individual, couple or family (usually no more) one lesson at a time for six weeks.

    1. The lessons are taught at a predetermined time mutually set by you and the student at the time the lessons are set up to be taught.

    2. The lessons are normally taught in the home of the student at his kitchen table. Sometimes a different location works better.

B. The lessons are systematic, not random. They begin at a certain point and develop toward a predetermined point in a definitely ordered structure.

155

1. They are taught in an informal setting which allows limited opportunity for questions and discussion. However the teaching is primarily an informal lecture with the teacher leading in a definite direction.

2. As you teach you will develop a chart which illustrates and defines what is being taught.

C. The nature of the six Bible lessons is twofold.

1. The first four lessons deal systematically with the plan of salvation and are designed to enable the student to understand the great work of God in Christ on his behalf. These lessons are designed to bring non-believing students to Christ.

2. The last two lessons deal systematically with discipleship. They show what should happen (and why) in a believer's life. They are designed to set him on the road to growth and maturity.

Section Two

Explain next that the training is designed to equip each trainee to set up and teach the *Basic Bible Truths* lessons.

A. Each trainee will be carefully taught the content of each of the six *Basic Bible Truths* lessons.

1. Fully written copies of each lesson should be provided for each trainee.

2. Verbal point by point explanations will be given during the training.

3. Once he completes the training, summary lesson plans in easy-to-follow outline form should be provided to each trainee for his own use in teaching.

B. Explain that the training course involves extensive actual teaching of the material by the trainee under monitored conditions. Help will be rendered until the trainee begins to gain confidence in teaching the material.

1. Explain that in the classroom the trainee will not be merely told how to do it and then be sent out to do it on his own.

2. To the contrary each trainee will first be paired with another trainee with whom he will practice teaching the lessons. This will occur after the nine week classroom period of learning the material.

After the practice phase with another trainee, each trainee will be matched with an experienced trainer whom the trainee will observe in an actual *in the field* teaching of the six lessons. That will be followed by the trainer observing the trainee teach an actual six lesson course *"in the field."*

Only then will consideration be given to the trainee becoming a teacher on his own as a part of the *Home Bible Studies Ministry*.

Section Three

Next explain what will be expected of trainees once the training is completed.

A. Upon completion of training each trainee will be expected to become an active part of the *Home Bible Studies Ministry* of the church.

1. Explain that the objective of this training is not merely an education on how to teach these lessons. The objective is to put more teachers in the field.

2. Upon completion of this training, each person will be expected to keep one *Basic Bible Truths* course in progress at all times. That means that at all time the person will either have a course in progress or be actively seeking to set up a course.

Our *Home Bible Studies Ministry* goal is for each teacher to teach at least six (6) courses per year. Doing so would require thirty-six weeks. The remaining sixteen weeks of the year would allow for vacations, sickness and the time necessary to seek out and set up new courses.

A teacher may desire to set up and teach more than six courses per year however no teacher in the ministry should teach less than six courses per year.

3. Normally the teacher will teach the *Basic Bible Truths* lessons one night per week at approximately 7:00 or 8:00 p.m. All classes cannot be arranged to fit that timing; arrange classes to fit opportunities. Teachers will be teaching Bible lessons at a variety of other times which are mutually acceptable between them and students.

B. As a teacher having completed the training, you should expect to work as a part of the church's *Home Bible Studies Ministry* and under the supervision of the director of that ministry. (Some churches will not have a ministry of this sort. If yours does not have one, go out and win as many souls as you possibly can.)

1. That will mean staying in weekly contact with the ministry director so that he will know who you are teaching, where you are in the lessons, what kind of results you have and when you are in need of a new student.

2. In some cases this may mean serving as a trainer for new trainees who come on the scene as new training courses are offered. If you are needed as a trainer, the ministry director will contact you.

3. Occasionally there will be joint meetings of all *Home Bible Study Ministry* personnel. You will be expected to attend these meetings, if at all possible. They will neither be more often than monthly nor less often than three times a year. Normally they will be every two months.

Section Four

Explain now that *Basic Bible Truths* training will consist of four (4) levels of training and will take about six (6) months to complete.

A. *Level one* training.

1. Level one consists of nine one-hour classroom sessions.

2. This is where the actual content of the six one-hour lessons is taught thoroughly.

B. *Level two* training.

1. This, too, is classroom activity and may take as little as six weeks or as much as twelve weeks to complete depending upon the initiative and available time of the given trainees.

2. At this point each trainee teaches the lessons to the trainee with whom he has been matched. If the trainees can give two hours per week during this level of training, it will be completed in six weeks. If the trainees can give only one hour each week, this level will require twelve weeks to complete.

   If the trainees can give two hours during this level, they should meet at the classroom where trainee #1 teaches trainee #2 the first lesson. As soon as trainee #1 finishes, trainee #2 then teaches him (trainee #1) the first lesson. The next week trainee #2 teaches first and they rotate back and forth through the six weeks.

   If the trainees can give only one hour weekly during this level, then trainee #1 first teaches lesson one to trainee #2. The following week trainee #2 teaches trainee #1 lesson one. The trainees rotate and follow this sequence through the twelve weeks.

3. The ministry director will supervise this level of training.

C. *Level three* training.

1. At this point each trainee will be assigned to an experienced trainer.

2. The trainee will go with the trainer and observe him actually setting up the course in an *in the field* situation. Then the trainee, as a silent partner, will accompany the trainer as he teaches the course. It is imperative that the trainee remain a *silent* partner during this level. Comments from an inexperienced trainee can seriously endanger the success of a course in a real life situation.

3. On the way to and returning from the lessons the trainer and trainee can discuss what is to be taught, teaching techniques, etc. This can be very helpful to the trainee.

D. *Level four* training.

1. The trainee continues with the assigned trainer through this level.

2. At this point the trainee and trainer go out together and the trainee sets up the Bible lessons with someone *in the field.* The trainer assumes the backup role. He goes with the trainee as the silent partner. On the way to and from the lessons he can coach the trainee. He is also there just in case the trainee should run into any kind of trouble.

3. This step may have to be repeated once especially the setup part. I suggest that in the event of a need to repeat the trainer go with the trainee, help him get the classes set up and then let the trainee go and do the actual teaching, on his own, without the trainer. By this point most trainees can do the teaching. It's the setup that gives them trouble.

4. Upon completion of level four training, the trainee becomes a certified member of the church's *Home Bible Studies Ministry* and begins to function as such.

Section Five

It is now time to explain exactly what should happen and is expected in level-one training.

A. First explain that each trainee will be matched with another trainee and that they will work together through level two training.

1. Explain that the trainees will be matched with someone they do not know very well. This helps them overcome their fear of meeting people they don't know.

2. Explain that each trainee will weekly hear the memory work and check the progress report sheet of his partner.

B. Explain next that each week study material will be given to each trainee.

1. It will consist of the title, thought and application of the coming lesson. It will also include the five memory verses associated with the coming lesson plus the lesson plan outline for that lesson.

2. Each trainee will be expected to memorize the title, thought and application of the appropriate lesson. He will also be required to memorize three of the five memory verses plus the Roman numeral headings from the outline. He will be expected to recite them to his trainee partner at next week's meeting.

C. Explain the nine one-hour sessions of level-one training.

1. Each hour will be divided into two segments with the exception of sessions eight and nine. The first segment will be fifteen minutes long. During that time matched trainees should be together reciting their memory work to each other. The appropriate boxes on the progress report sheets should be checked.

   The second segment will be forty-five minutes long. During this segment your instructor will teach you point-by-point how to teach each of the six lessons. You will be given full printed copies of each lesson for your own study and notations. These will be of great help later when you are actually teaching the classes to others.

2. The nine one-hour sessions of level-one training are arranged as follows:

   a. Session 1 - The orientation contained in this chapter.

   b. Session 2 - Memory work and how to teach lesson 1.

   c. Session 3 - Memory work and how to teach lesson 2.

   d. Session 4 - Test, memory work and how to teach lesson 3.

   e. Session 5 - Memory work and how to teach lesson 4.

   f. Session 6 - Test, memory work and how to teach lesson 5.

   g. Session 7 - Memory work and how to teach lesson 6.

   h. Session 8 - Teaching techniques.

   i. Session 9 - The final test.

161

D. Explain that there will be three tests in level-one training.

1. The first test will be at the beginning of session four. Each trainee will be asked to write down the titles, thoughts and applications of the first two lessons. Each trainee will also be asked to write down any three of the ten possible memory verses from lessons one and two. Each trainee will also be asked to write down the major Roman numeral points, in proper order, of both lessons one and two.

2. The second test will be at the beginning of session six. Each trainee will be asked to write down the titles, thoughts and applications of lessons three and four. Each trainee will also be asked to write down any three of the ten possible memory verses from lessons three and four. Each trainee will also be asked to write down the major Roman numeral points, in proper order, of both lessons three and four outlines.

3. The third and final test will be given during session nine. Each trainee will be asked to write down the titles, thoughts and applications of both lessons five and six. He will also be asked to write down three of the possible ten memory verses associated with lessons five and six. He will be asked to write down, in proper order, the major Roman numeral points of both lessons five and six. He will also be asked to construct the chart using his notes to aid him.

Section Six

Conclude this and each training session by:

A. Handing out the proper study sheets for next week.

B. Matching trainees into pairs for the above mentioned study purposes.

A SPECIAL WORD

It is my hope and prayer that you will wisely and boldly use this tool to bring many to Christ as well as strengthen those in Him who are weak.

About the Author

LESTER HUTSON served as a Baptist pastor for over 60 years. He has also served as a national field representative for the Christian Law Association, a conference and revival speaker and the author of numerous books. He is committed to first-century Christianity, the inerrancy of the Scriptures and personal evangelism.

www.lesterhutson.org

Made in the USA
Coppell, TX
28 January 2020

15110560R00095